TROPHIES

Spelling Practice Book

Teacher's Edition

Grade 3

Harcourt

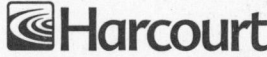

Orlando Boston Dallas Chicago San Diego

Visit *The Learning Site!*

www.harcourtschool.com

REPRODUCING COPIES FOR STUDENTS

This Teacher's Edition contains full-size student pages with answers printed in non-reproducible blue ink.

It may be necessary to adjust the exposure control on your photocopy machine to a lighter setting to ensure that blue answers do not reproduce.

ISBN 0-15-323552-7

8 9 10   082   10 09 08 07 06 05 04

Contents

Contents

Theme 5

Theme 6

Making Your Spelling Log

This book gives you a place to keep a word list of your own. It's called a **SPELLING LOG!**

If you need some **IDEAS** for creating your list, just look at what I usually do!

While I read, I look for words that I think are **INTERESTING.** I listen for **NEW WORDS** used by people on radio and television.

I include words that I need to use when I **WRITE,** especially words that are hard for me to spell.

Before I write a word in my Spelling Log, I check the spelling. I look up the word in a **DICTIONARY** or a **THESAURUS,** or I ask for help.

To help me understand and remember the meaning of my word, I write a **DEFINITION,** a **SYNONYM,** or an **ANTONYM.** I also use my word in a sentence.

Making Your Spelling Log

Here's how you use it!

THE SPELLING LOG SECTION of this book is just for you. It's your own list of words that you want to remember. Your Spelling Log has three parts. Here's how to use each part.

Spelling Words to Study

This is where you'll list words from each lesson that you need to study. Include words you misspell on the Pretest and any other words you aren't sure you can always spell correctly.

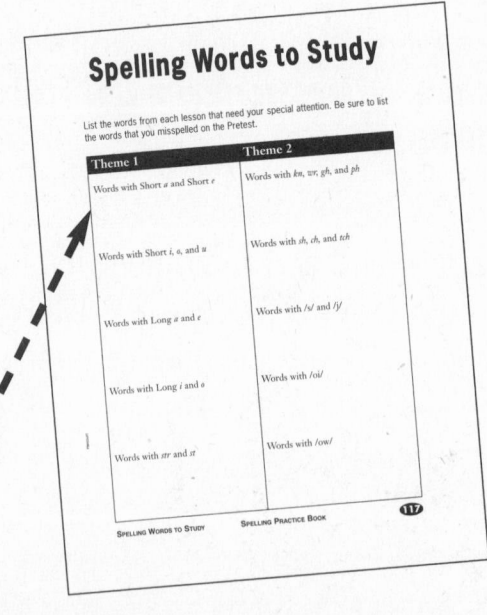

This handy list makes it easy for me to study the words I need to learn!

Harcourt

Making Your Spelling Log

I write a clue beside each word to help me remember it.

My Own Word Collection

You choose the words to list on these pages. Include new words, interesting words, and any other words you want to remember. You decide how to group them, too!

Harcourt

Study Steps to Learn a Word

Check out these steps.

SAY
THE WORD.

Remember when you have heard the word used. Think about what it means.

2

LOOK
AT THE WORD.

Find any prefixes, suffixes, or other word parts you know. Think of another word that is related in meaning and spelling. Try to picture the word in your mind.

Harcourt

SPELL
THE WORD TO YOURSELF.

Think about the way each sound is spelled. Notice any unusual letter combinations.

WRITE
THE WORD WHILE YOU ARE LOOKING AT IT.

Check the way you have formed your letters. If you have not written the word clearly or correctly, write it again.

CHECK
WHAT YOU HAVE LEARNED.

Cover the word and write it. If you have not spelled the word correctly, practice these steps until you can write it correctly every time.

Harcourt

SPELLING WORDS

1. sat
2. felt
3. last
4. send
5. next
6. best
7. went
8. hand
9. stand
10. past
11. grand
12. stamp
13. belt
14. lend
15. checked

Words with Short *a* and Short *e*

▶ Write the Spelling Word that matches the meaning.

1. a strap to hold up pants _____ belt

2. touched _____ felt

3. looked over _____ checked

4. to be up on your feet _____ stand

5. to let someone borrow _____ lend

6. postage for a letter _____ stamp

▶ Write the Spelling Word that is the opposite of the given word.

7. receive _____ send

8. worst _____ best

9. present _____ past

10. stayed _____ went

11. last _____ first

▶ Write the following Spelling Words: *sat, last, hand, grand.* Use your best handwriting.

12. _____ sat   14. _____ hand

13. _____ last   15. _____ grand

Handwriting Tip: Complete the down stroke in the letter *a*, so it does not look like an *o*.

Harcourt

Name_____

▶ For each pair, circle the word that is not spelled correctly. Check the spelling. Then write each misspelled Spelling Word correctly.

1. (seand)   went   ___send___

2. stand   (hend)   ___hand___

3. (feelt)   next   ___felt___

4. sat   (lahst)   ___last___

▶ Read the letter. Circle six words that do not look right. Check the spelling. Then write the misspelled words correctly.

> August 10
> Dear Connie,
>   Today was the (behst!) I (weant) to camp for the first time. All my fears about camp are in the (paast.) The food is (grannd,) and I had fun trying to (stahnd) on my hands. I can't wait to paddle a canoe. That's (naxt!)
>   Your friend,
>   Phil

5. ___best___   8. ___grand___

6. ___went___   9. ___stand___

7. ___past___   10. ___next___

SPELLING WORDS

1. sat
2. felt
3. last
4. send
5. next
6. best
7. went
8. hand
9. stand
10. past
11. grand
12. stamp
13. belt
14. lend
15. checked

SPELLING STRATEGY

Checking Twice

When you proofread, circle words that do not look right. Check your work twice to be sure you have not missed any mistakes.

Harcourt

SPELLING WORDS

1. sat
2. felt
3. last
4. send
5. next
6. best
7. went
8. hand
9. stand
10. past
11. grand
12. stamp
13. belt
14. lend
15. checked

▶ **Try It Out** Write a Spelling Word for each clue.

1. This word has five letters, has short *a*, and rhymes with <u>damp</u>. stamp

2. This word has four letters, has short *e*, and rhymes with <u>bend</u>. send

3. This word has four letters, has short *a*, and rhymes with <u>band</u>. hand

4. This word has four letters, has short *e*, and rhymes with <u>rest</u>. best

5. This word has seven letters, has short *e*, and rhymes with <u>pecked</u>. checked

▶ **Word Search** Find and circle three Spelling Words with short *a* and three Spelling Words with short *e*. Write each word under the correct heading. Order may vary.

q	k	w	n	x	p
h	r	b	e	l	t
p	z	c	x	e	g
u	d	l	t	n	f
g	r	a	n	d	o
w	e	s	h	f	g
s	a	t	b	x	r

Short a

6. grand
7. last
8. sat

Short e

9. next
10. belt
11. lend

Harcourt

Name _____

Words with Short *i*, *o*, and *u*

▶ Write the Spelling Word that means the same
or nearly the same as the given word.

1. pool   _pond_____
2. hop   _jump_____
3. plate   _dish_____
4. stones   _rocks_____
5. choose   _pick_____
6. knock   _thump_____

▶ Write a Spelling Word for each clue.

7. the opposite of *to*   _from_____
8. an animal that lives in water   _fish_____
9. worn on the feet   _socks_____
10. a large automobile   _truck_____
11. the second meal of the day   _lunch_____

▶ Write the following Spelling Words: *thing, slip,
inch, gift*. Use your best handwriting.

12. _thing_____   14. _inch_____
13. _slip_____   15. _gift_____

SPELLING WORDS

1. slip
2. fish
3. pick
4. rocks
5. lunch
6. gift
7. thing
8. inch
9. truck
10. pond
11. from
12. jump
13. socks
14. dish
15. thump

**Handwriting
Tip:** Be careful
the letter *i* does
not go above
the midline, or
it could look
like the letter *l*.

Harcourt

SPELLING WORDS

1. slip
2. fish
3. pick
4. rocks
5. lunch
6. gift
7. thing
8. inch
9. truck
10. pond
11. from
12. jump
13. socks
14. dish
15. thump

SPELLING STRATEGY

Comparing Spellings

When you're not sure how to spell a word, try writing it in different ways. Then choose the spelling that looks correct.

▶ **Look at the two possible spellings. Circle the word that is misspelled. Then write the Spelling Word that is correct.**

1. socks   (soks)   _socks_
2. (frum)   from   _from_
3. thump   (thomp)   _thump_
4. inch   (ench)   _inch_
5. dish   (desh)   _dish_
6. (slep)   slip   _slip_

▶ **Complete the postcard. Circle the correct spelling. Then write each Spelling Word.**

Dear Ben,

   We rode to the (**pond**, pawnd) in my uncle's (trock, **truck**). The (fesh, **fish**) swim near the big (rawcks, **rocks**). Sometimes I can see them (**jump**, jomp) out of the water. I love to eat them for (lonch, **lunch**)!

   Your friend,
   Casey

7. _pond_   10. _rocks_
8. _truck_   11. _jump_
9. _fish_   12. _lunch_

Harcourt

Name _____

▶ **Complete the Poem** Write Spelling Words to complete the silly poem. Use the underlined word in each pair of lines as a hint.

Carrots in a <u>bunch</u>

Ryan eats for **(1)** ___lunch___ .

In his purple <u>socks</u>

Ryan jumps on **(2)** ___rocks___ .

Nancy got <u>stuck</u>

In her father's **(3)** ___truck___ .

Maria got her <u>wish</u>—

She caught a great big **(4)** ___fish___ .

▶ **Rhyme Time!** On each line, write a Spelling Word that rhymes with the underlined word.

5. The boat began to <u>drift</u>. ___gift___

6. Manuel is <u>fond</u> of cats. ___pond___

7. Kerry can do a <u>flip</u>. ___slip___

8. We are going to <u>come</u> home now. ___from___

9. My rabbit likes to <u>munch</u> carrots. ___lunch___

10. That clock has a loud <u>tick</u>. ___pick___

11. My new shoes <u>pinch</u> my toes. ___inch___

12. Did you hear the phone <u>ring</u>? ___thing___

Harcourt

SPELLING WORDS

1. easy
2. grade
3. meet
4. late
5. seat
6. saved
7. pail
8. these
9. reach
10. name
11. raise
12. leave
13. gain
14. theme
15. scream

Handwriting Tip: Close up an *e*, so it does not look like a *c*.

Words with Long *a* and *e*

▶ Write the Spelling Word that is the opposite of the given word.

1. lose _____gain_____

2. early _____late_____

3. whisper _____scream_____

4. hard _____easy_____

5. lower _____raise_____

6. those _____these_____

7. arrive _____leave_____

▶ Write the Spelling Word from the box that best completes each sentence.

name	pail	saved	grade

8. *Maria* is her first _____name_____.

9. Next year I will be in fourth _____grade_____.

10. The farmer's _____pail_____ is full of milk.

11. Mike _____saved_____ five dollars in his bank.

▶ Write the following Spelling Words: *theme, seat, reach, meet.* Use your best handwriting.

12. _____theme_____   14. _____reach_____

13. _____seat_____   15. _____meet_____

Harcourt

Name _____

▶ **Work with a partner to circle the five Spelling Words that do not look right to you. Write the correct spelling for each one.**

1. (graid)   grade   _____grade_____

2. gain   (gane)   _____gain_____

3. (sete)   seat   _____seat_____

4. (theas)   these   _____these_____

5. (screme)   scream   _____scream_____

6. raise   (raize)   _____raise_____

▶ **Read the letter with a partner. Circle the six misspelled words. Then write the correct spellings on the lines below.**

Dear Matt,
   It took two hours to (reche) the lake. Each morning we (rase) the flag. We went fishing (lait) in the day. We put our bait in a (pale) of water. It is (eesy) to catch fish here. I don't ever want to (leve)!

                    Your friend,
                    Jennifer

7. _____reach_____   10. _____pail_____

8. _____raise_____   11. _____easy_____

9. _____late_____   12. _____leave_____

SPELLING WORDS

1. easy
2. grade
3. meet
4. late
5. seat
6. saved
7. pail
8. these
9. reach
10. name
11. raise
12. leave
13. gain
14. theme
15. scream

SPELLING STRATEGY

Working Together

When you proofread, work with a partner. Read the words aloud as your partner looks at the spelling. Then switch jobs.

Harcourt

Name_____

SPELLING WORDS

1. easy
2. grade
3. meet
4. late
5. seat
6. saved
7. pail
8. these
9. reach
10. name
11. raise
12. leave
13. gain
14. theme
15. scream

▶ **Try It Out** Add the letters that spell the vowel sounds to write Spelling Words. Then write the words.

1. m__e__ __e__ t _____meet_____

2. gr__a__d__e__ _____grade_____

3. r__a__ __i__ s__e__ _____raise_____

4. th__e__ m__e__ _____theme_____

5. l__e__ __a__ v__e__ _____leave_____

6. __e__ __a__ sy _____easy_____

7. s__a__ v__e__ d _____saved_____

▶ **Rhyme Time!** On each line, write a Spelling Word that rhymes with the underlined word.

8. Stretch and ____reach____ for the <u>peach</u>.

9. "Marco Polo" is the ____name____ of a <u>game</u>.

10. When I <u>sail</u>, I bring my ____pail____.

11. Inez is ____late____ for our play <u>date</u>.

12. Take a ____seat____ near the <u>heat</u>.

Harcourt

Name _____

Words with Long *i* and *o*

▶ **Write the Spelling Word that matches the meaning.**

1. cracked in pieces _____ broke _____

2. during the same time _____ while _____

3. go in the same direction _____ follow _____

4. under _____ below _____

5. the act of flying _____ flight _____

6. full of light _____ bright _____

▶ **Write a Spelling Word to complete each sentence.**

7. I looked out the _____ window _____.

8. At what _____ time _____ does school begin?

9. These old pants are too _____ tight _____.

10. Sun helps plants _____ grow _____.

11. The ocean's _____ tide _____ is high.

▶ **Write the following Spelling Words: *show,*** ***stone, whole, close.* Use your best handwriting.**

12. _____ show _____   14. _____ whole _____

13. _____ stone _____   15. _____ close _____

SPELLING WORDS

1. tight
2. while
3. show
4. stone
5. bright
6. whole
7. window
8. time
9. follow
10. close
11. flight
12. tide
13. grow
14. broke
15. below

Handwriting Tip: Make sure the letter *o* does not look like an *a*.

Harcourt

SPELLING WORDS

1. tight
2. while
3. show
4. stone
5. bright
6. whole
7. window
8. time
9. follow
10. close
11. flight
12. tide
13. grow
14. broke
15. below

SPELLING STRATEGY

Rhyming Words

Think about the sound of a word. Does it rhyme with a word you know? Use the spelling pattern of the rhyming word to try to spell the word.

▶ **Circle the Spelling Word or Words that rhyme with the underlined word in each row. Then write the rhyming words below.** Order may vary.

<u>hose</u>	(close)	noise	choose
<u>light</u>	(bright)	chief	(tight)
<u>lime</u>	field	(time)	lip
<u>blow</u>	(show)	house	(grow)

1. ____close____   4. ____time____

2. ____bright____   5. ____show____

3. ____tight____   6. ____grow____

▶ **Circle the six misspelled words in the journal entry. Then write the Spelling Words correctly.**

(Wile) I was at the beach, the (tyde) was high. I climbed up on a huge (stoane) and watched as the waves (broake) on the shore. Then a (hoal) flock of birds flew overhead. I wanted to (follough) them.

7. ____While____   10. ____broke____

8. ____tide____   11. ____whole____

9. ____stone____   12. ____follow____

SPELLING PRACTICE BOOK

LESSON 4

Name _____

▶ **Complete the Poem** Write rhyming Spelling Words to finish the poem.

Sue and Pat each have a dime,

They're at the theater right on **(1)** ___time___ .

But Sue and Pat didn't know.

It's the day of the magic **(2)** ___show___ !

Sue's frown becomes a smile.

The wait was worth her **(3)** ___while___ .

Sue calls her brother on the phone.

"I just saw water turned to **(4)** ___stone___ !"

▶ **Change-a-Word** Add and subtract letters from the words below to write Spelling Words.

5. c + lose = ___close___

6. w + holes – s = ___whole___

7. windy – y + ow = ___window___

8. fol + slow – s = ___follow___

9. be + low = ___below___

10. bright – br + fl = ___flight___

11. crime – cr + t = ___time___

12. g + row = ___grow___

SPELLING WORDS

1. tight
2. while
3. show
4. stone
5. bright
6. whole
7. window
8. time
9. follow
10. close
11. flight
12. tide
13. grow
14. broke
15. below

Words with *str* and *st*

SPELLING WORDS

1. least
2. fast
3. just
4. burst
5. strip
6. stick
7. strike
8. artist
9. almost
10. student
11. strong
12. start
13. blast
14. step
15. street

► Write the Spelling Words that mean the same or nearly the same as the given words.

1. begin   _____start_____

2. nearly   _____almost_____

3. hit   _____strike_____

4. quick   _____fast_____

5. roar   _____blast_____

6. road   _____street_____

► Write a Spelling Word for each clue.

7. This is someone who paints.   _____artist_____

8. This is someone who goes to school.   _____student_____

9. This is a small tree branch.   _____stick_____

10. A balloon with too much air will do this.   _____burst_____

11. To move one foot forward.   _____step_____

► Write the following Spelling Words: *least, just, strip, strong*. Use your best handwriting.

12. _____least_____   14. _____strip_____

13. _____just_____   15. _____strong_____

Handwriting Tip: When writing *st*, be sure the *t* does not look like an *l*.

st

Harcourt

Name _____

▶ Look at each pair of spellings. Circle the word that is misspelled. Then check the word list, and write the correct spelling for each Spelling Word.

SPELLING WORDS

1. stick   (sitck)   _stick_
2. (almots) almost   _almost_
3. (artis)   artist   _artist_
4. (srtike) strike   _strike_
5. least   (leas)   _least_
6. (sudent) student   _student_
7. (stepp)   step   _step_
8. strip   (srtip)   _strip_

SPELLING WORDS

1. least
2. fast
3. just
4. burst
5. strip
6. stick
7. strike
8. artist
9. almost
10. student
11. strong
12. start
13. blast
14. step
15. street

▶ Read each pair of words. Circle the word that is misspelled. Then complete the sentence by writing the word correctly on the line.

(juts) just

9. There are ___just___ two crayons left.

fast (fats)

10. My bike is ___fast___ .

(burts) burst

11. Look! My balloon has ___burst___ .

strong (stong)

12. Milk helps build ___strong___ bones.

SPELLING STRATEGY

Guessing and Checking

When you are not sure how to spell a word, make a guess. Then check to see whether your spelling is correct.

Harcourt

SPELLING WORDS

1. least
2. fast
3. just
4. burst
5. strip
6. stick
7. strike
8. artist
9. almost
10. student
11. strong
12. start
13. blast
14. step
15. street

▶ **Try It Out** Add the letters *str* or *st* and then write the Spelling Word.

1. bur__s__ __t__ _____ burst

2. __s__ __t__ __r__ eet _____ street

3. fa__s__ __t__ _____ fast

4. __s__ __t__ __r__ ip _____ strip

5. ju__s__ __t__ _____ just

6. __s__ __t__ ep _____ step

▶ **Smaller Words** Write the Spelling Words that have these smaller words in them.

7. ends with <u>most</u> _____ almost

8. begins with <u>star</u> _____ start

9. ends with <u>rip</u> _____ strip

10. begins with <u>art</u> _____ artist

11. ends with <u>last</u> _____ blast

12. ends with <u>dent</u> _____ student

13. ends with <u>tick</u> _____ stick

14. ends with <u>east</u> _____ least

Harcourt

Practice Test

▶ **Read each sentence. Fill in the oval next to the correctly spelled word that completes each sentence.**

1. We _____ to the beach last week.

   ⬭ wint   ⬭ weant   ⬬ went

2. He writes with his left _____.

   ⬬ hand   ⬭ haind   ⬭ hend

3. It was my turn at _____.

   ⬭ lasst   ⬭ laist   ⬬ last

4. My dad _____ my math homework.

   ⬬ checked   ⬭ chacked   ⬭ chicked

5. A man will _____ your ticket at the gate.

   ⬭ stemp   ⬭ stimp   ⬬ stamp

6. She caught a big _____ at the lake.

   ⬬ fish   ⬭ fesh   ⬭ fush

7. An _____ of snow fell today.

   ⬭ ench   ⬭ anch   ⬬ inch

8. We saw a turtle in the _____.

   ⬭ pund   ⬬ pond   ⬭ pand

9. He likes to _____ on rocks.

   ⬬ jump   ⬭ jamp   ⬭ jomp

10. They walked _____ their house to the park.

    ⬭ frum   ⬬ from   ⬭ frem

Harcourt

Name _____

▶ **Read each sentence. The underlined word is misspelled. Fill in the oval next to the correct spelling.**

1. He <u>saived</u> a place for me in line.
   ⬭ sayved ⬬ saved ⬭ saeved

2. Have you read any of <u>thees</u> books?
   ⬬ these ⬭ thease ⬭ theese

3. You will <u>gane</u> ten points for each right answer.
   ⬭ gayne ⬭ gean ⬬ gain

4. I like <u>brite</u> colors.
   ⬭ britte ⬬ bright ⬭ bryte

5. His boots felt too <u>tyte</u>.
   ⬭ tiet ⬭ tite ⬬ tight

6. What <u>tim</u> does the game start?
   ⬭ tyme ⬭ tighm ⬬ time

7. Will you <u>chowe</u> me the way back?
   ⬬ show ⬭ showe ⬭ shoa

8. They painted the <u>hoal</u> fence.
   ⬭ whol ⬬ whole ⬭ whowl

9. They live in the apartment <u>belowe</u> us.
   ⬬ below ⬭ beloaw ⬭ belo

10. Can you <u>strick</u> the nail with this hammer?
    ⬬ strike ⬭ streike ⬭ srike

Harcourt

Words with *kn, wr, gh,* and *ph*

SPELLING WORDS

1. known
2. written
3. laugh
4. sphere
5. wreck
6. writer
7. wrong
8. wrap
9. wrench
10. knocked
11. knot
12. wring
13. enough
14. rough
15. wrinkle

▶ **Write a Spelling Word for each clue.**

1. incorrect ___wrong___

2. tangle ___knot___

3. a car accident ___wreck___

4. squeeze ___wring___

5. an author ___writer___

6. crinkle or crumple ___wrinkle___

7. tapped, as on a door ___knocked___

8. to cover with paper ___wrap___

9. a tool ___wrench___

▶ **Write the Spelling Word that best completes each sentence.**

10. Have you ___written___ your report?

11. I would have made cookies if I had ___known___ you were coming.

▶ **Write the following Spelling Words: *laugh, sphere, enough,* and *rough.* Use your best handwriting.**

12. ___laugh___   14. ___enough___

13. ___sphere___   15. ___rough___

Handwriting Tip: When writing an *h*, make sure it is open and not closed, so it does not look like a *b*.

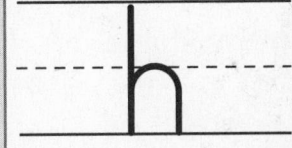

Harcourt

SPELLING WORDS

1. known
2. written
3. laugh
4. sphere
5. wreck
6. writer
7. wrong
8. wrap
9. wrench
10. knocked
11. knot
12. wring
13. enough
14. rough
15. wrinkle

SPELLING STRATEGY

Word Shapes

To remember the spelling of a word, draw its shape. Then when you write the word, think of its shape.

▶ **Write the Spelling Word that fits in each word shape.**

1.

2.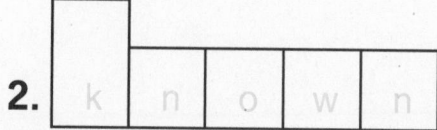

3.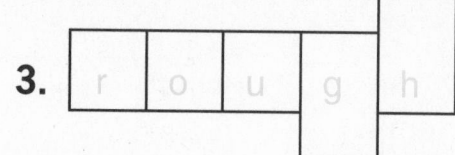

4.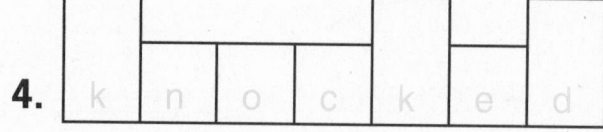

5.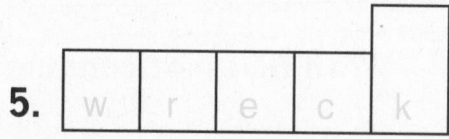

▶ **Write the Spelling Words to complete the sentences.**

6. I like to _____ laugh _____ at jokes.

7. There is a _____ wrinkle _____ in my shirt.

8. Do you have _____ enough _____ money saved?

9. Did you _____ wrap _____ her present?

10. Tie a _____ knot _____ in the rope.

11. The globe is shaped like a _____ sphere _____.

Harcourt

Name_____

▶ **Try It Out** Add letters to complete the Spelling Words. Then write the words.

1. __w__ __r__ itten   _written_

2. lau __g__ __h__   _laugh_

3. __k__ __n__ ot   _knot_

4. __w__ __r__ ing   _wring_

▶ **Word Puzzle** Write Spelling Words to complete this puzzle. Use the clues to help you.

ACROSS

5. an author
6. not right
7. rhymes with *grown*
8. round, like the earth

DOWN

9. a tool for fixing things
10. parts of a ship on a beach
11. what you do to a gift

SPELLING WORDS

1. known
2. written
3. laugh
4. sphere
5. wreck
6. writer
7. wrong
8. wrap
9. wrench
10. knocked
11. knot
12. wring
13. enough
14. rough
15. wrinkle

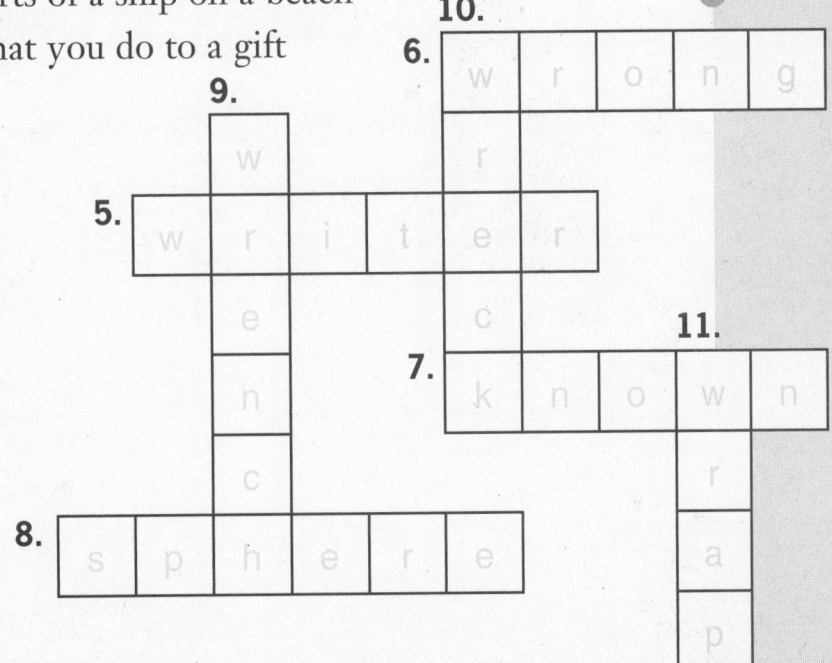

Harcourt

SPELLING WORDS

1. shot
2. chance
3. match
4. watch
5. showed
6. shock
7. pushed
8. such
9. crash
10. chew
11. batch
12. hitched
13. sharp
14. mush
15. speech

Handwriting Tip: Be sure not to slant your letters when you write.

Words with *sh, ch,* and *tch*

▶ Write a Spelling Word to complete each sentence.

1. That loud noise gave me

   quite a ___shock___ .

2. Have you ever heard ___such___ a racket?

3. Let's make a ___batch___ of cookies.

▶ Put these words in alphabetical order.

match	showed	crash	watch
chew	sharp	pushed	speech

4. ___chew___   8. ___sharp___

5. ___crash___   9. ___showed___

6. ___match___   10. ___speech___

7. ___pushed___   11. ___watch___

▶ Write the following Spelling Words: *shot, chance, hitched,* and *mush.* Use your best handwriting.

12. ___shot___   14. ___hitched___

13. ___chance___   15. ___mush___

Harcourt

Name _____

▶ **Circle the letters that complete the Spelling Words. Write the words.**

One stormy night, Dad and I were making a ba(**ch**, **tch**) of bread. We heard a (**sh**, **sch**)arp rap on the door. Dad looked at his wa(**ch**, **tch**). "Who could that be at su(**ch**, **tch**) a late hour?" he asked. Next the lights went out. Dad lit a ma(**ch**, **tch**). Then the door flew open. I was scared until Dad said that a gust of wind had pu(**sht**, **shed**) it open.

1. _____batch_____   4. _____such_____

2. _____sharp_____   5. _____match_____

3. _____watch_____   6. _____pushed_____

▶ **Write the Spelling Words you would find on a dictionary page with *shoal* and *showy* as guide words.**

7. _____shock_____

8. _____shot_____

9. _____showed_____

▶ **Write the Spelling Words you would find on a dictionary page with *champ* and *crate* as guide words.**

10. _____chance_____

11. _____chew_____

12. _____crash_____

SPELLING WORDS

1. shot
2. chance
3. match
4. watch
5. showed
6. shock
7. pushed
8. such
9. crash
10. chew
11. batch
12. hitched
13. sharp
14. mush
15. speech

SPELLING STRATEGIES

Dictionary

Guide words tell the first and last entry words on the page of a dictionary.

Harcourt

SPELLING WORDS

1. shot
2. chance
3. match
4. watch
5. showed
6. shock
7. pushed
8. such
9. crash
10. chew
11. batch
12. hitched
13. sharp
14. mush
15. speech

▶ **Try It Out** Add letters to complete the Spelling Words. Then write the words.

1. __s__ __h__ ock   shock

2. pu__s__ __h__ ed   pushed

3. ma__t__ __c__ __h__   match

4. mu__s__ __h__   mush

5. spee__c__ __h__   speech

6. hi__t__ __c__ __h__ ed   hitched

▶ **Use the Clues** Write a Spelling Word for each clue.

7. This word has six letters, has the letter *a*, and rhymes with <u>dance</u>.   chance

8. This word has four letters, has the letter *u*, and rhymes with <u>much</u>.   such

9. This word has five letters, has the letter *a*, and rhymes with <u>notch</u>.   watch

10. This word has six letters, has the letter *o*, and rhymes with <u>snowed</u>.   showed

11. This word has four letters, has the letter *e*, and rhymes with <u>blew</u>.   chew

12. This word has four letters, has the letter *o*, and rhymes with <u>not</u>.   shot

Harcourt

Name _____

Words with /s/ and /j/

▶ Write the Spelling Word that matches each picture.

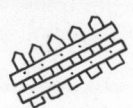  

1. __fence__ 3. __police__ 5. __price__

2. __stage__ 4. __giraffe__ 6. __pencil__

▶ Write the Spelling Word that matches each word or group of words.

7. to make someone do something __force__

8. where astronauts go __space__

9. a room for doing work __office__

10. to thrill __excite__

11. a motor __engine__

▶ Write the following Spelling Words: *ginger*, *badge*, *range*, and *huge*. Use your best handwriting.

12. __ginger__ 14. __range__

13. __badge__ 15. __huge__

SPELLING WORDS
1. space
2. stage
3. huge
4. fence
5. price
6. police
7. office
8. engine
9. badge
10. pencil
11. excite
12. force
13. range
14. ginger
15. giraffe

Handwriting Tip: Be sure the letter *g* does not look like a *q*.

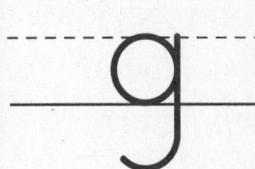

Harcourt

SPELLING WORDS

1. space
2. stage
3. huge
4. fence
5. price
6. police
7. office
8. engine
9. badge
10. pencil
11. excite
12. force
13. range
14. ginger
15. giraffe

SPELLING STRATEGY

Classifying Errors

When you proofread, keep a list of your spelling errors. Notice the kinds of mistakes you usually make. Look out for these kinds of errors in your work.

▶ **What's wrong with each word in the box? Follow the directions to write the Spelling Words correctly.**

Order may vary.

| jinjer spaec exsite fense ranje priec |

Change the consonant *s* to correct two words.
Change the consonant *j* to correct two words.
Reverse two letters to correct two words.

1. _____fence_____   4. _____range_____

2. _____excite_____   5. _____space_____

3. _____ginger_____   6. _____price_____

▶ **Read Kevin's report. Circle six words that do not look right. Check the spelling. Then write the misspelled words correctly.**

On Friday's field trip, we visited a polic station. There was a huj offise with computers and a short-wave radio. We signed our names with a weird pensil before we left. We met several nice officers who are on the fors. One of them showed us her baj.

7. _____police_____   10. _____pencil_____

8. _____huge_____   11. _____force_____

9. _____office_____   12. _____badge_____

Harcourt

Name _____

▶ **Fun with Words** Proofread the tongue twisters. Circle the spelling error in each one. Then write the misspelled words correctly.

SPELLING WORDS

1. space
2. stage
3. huge
4. fence
5. price
6. police
7. office
8. engine
9. badge
10. pencil
11. excite
12. force
13. range
14. ginger
15. giraffe

1. Fred found five fresh fish on a (fense).

fence

2. An enormous (enjine) pulled an elephant easily.

engine

3. Prince Paul paid a pretty (prise) for the plump puppies.

price

4. Pretty Polly Parrot went patrolling with the (polise).

police

5. The odd octopus opened an (offise) in October.

office

6. George the (jiraffe) is a genuinely gentle giant.

giraffe

7. Reindeer roam the (ranje) near the Rusty-R Ranch.

range

▶ **Word Groups** Write the Spelling Word that best fits with each group of words.

8. small, large, tiny, _huge_

9. eraser, paper, pen, _pencil_

10. play, scene, actor, _stage_

11. rocket, planet, stars, _space_

Harcourt

SPELLING WORDS

1. joyful
2. choice
3. voice
4. joint
5. moist
6. spoil
7. royal
8. annoy
9. noise
10. employ
11. soil
12. loyal
13. boiled
14. destroy
15. pointy

Words with /oi/

► Write a Spelling Word for each clue.

1. used in speaking _____ voice
2. like a king or queen _____ royal
3. a loud sound _____ noise
4. to hire for work _____ employ
5. slightly wet _____ moist
6. to wreck something completely _____ destroy
7. very happy _____ joyful

► Write the Spelling Word that means the same or nearly the same as the given word.

8. bother _____ annoy
9. rot _____ spoil
10. sharp _____ pointy
11. faithful _____ loyal

► Write the following Spelling Words: *choice, joint, soil* and *boiled*. Use your best handwriting.

12. _____ choice   14. _____ soil
13. _____ joint   15. _____ boiled

Handwriting Tip: Make sure your *i*s don't look like *l*s.

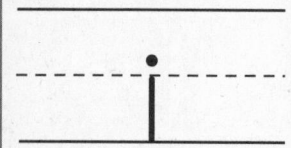

Harcourt

Name _____

▶ **Look at the two possible spellings. Circle the words that are misspelled. Then write the Spelling Word that is correct.**

1. voice (voyce) _____voice_____

2. (soyl) soil _____soil_____

3. (annoi) annoy _____annoy_____

4. noise (noyse) _____noise_____

5. (roial) royal _____royal_____

6. employ (emploi) _____employ_____

7. pointy (poynty) _____pointy_____

8. (boyled) boiled _____boiled_____

SPELLING WORDS

1. joyful
2. choice
3. voice
4. joint
5. moist
6. spoil
7. royal
8. annoy
9. noise
10. employ
11. soil
12. loyal
13. boiled
14. destroy
15. pointy

▶ **Read the diary entry. Circle the six misspelled words. Then write the correct spellings.**

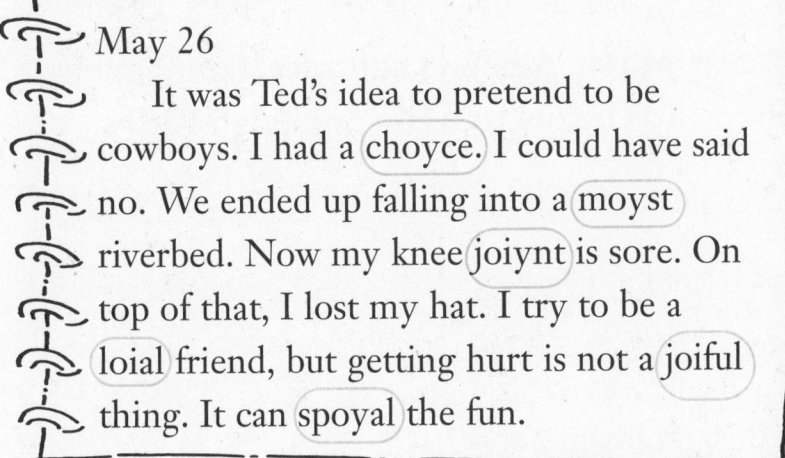

May 26
    It was Ted's idea to pretend to be cowboys. I had a (choyce.) I could have said no. We ended up falling into a (moyst) riverbed. Now my knee (joiynt) is sore. On top of that, I lost my hat. I try to be a (loial) friend, but getting hurt is not a (joiful) thing. It can (spoyal) the fun.

SPELLING STRATEGY

Using a Dictionary

Use a dictionary to correct misspelled words. Use guide words to find words quickly.

9. _____choice_____   12. _____loyal_____

10. _____moist_____   13. _____joyful_____

11. _____joint_____   14. _____spoil_____

Harcourt

SPELLING WORDS

1. joyful
2. choice
3. voice
4. joint
5. moist
6. spoil
7. royal
8. annoy
9. noise
10. employ
11. soil
12. loyal
13. boiled
14. destroy
15. pointy

▶ **Name That Word** Draw a line to connect the Spelling Word to its clue. Then write the word on the line below.

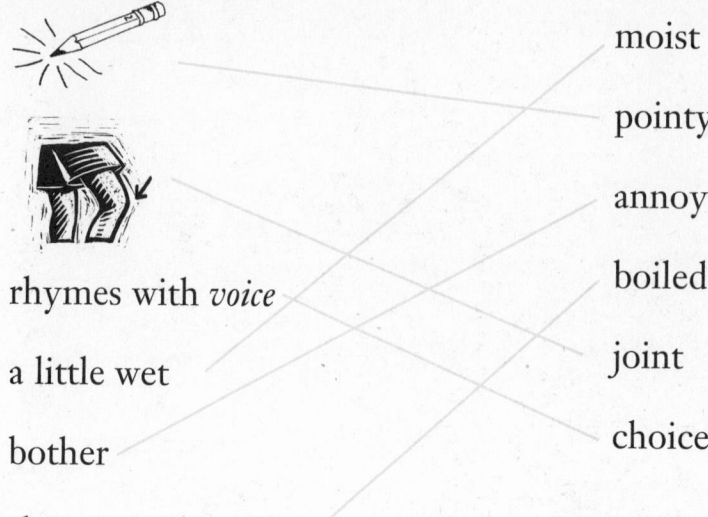

moist

pointy

annoy

boiled

joint

choice

rhymes with *voice*

a little wet

bother

rhymes with *spoiled*

1. _____pointy_____   4. _____moist_____

2. _____joint_____   5. _____annoy_____

3. _____choice_____   6. _____boiled_____

▶ **Word Math** Add and subtract letters from the words below to write Spelling Words.

7. dew – w + stroy = _____destroy_____

8. void – d + ce = _____voice_____

9. no + ise = _____noise_____

10. employer – er = _____employ_____

11. row – w + yal = _____royal_____

12. join + t = _____joint_____

13. cho + ice = _____choice_____

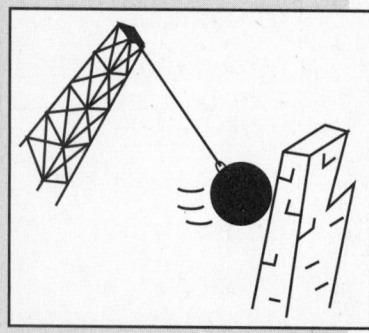

Harcourt

Name _____

Words with /ou/

▶ **Write a Spelling Word to complete each sentence.**

1. Ms. Wang is _____proud_____ of her class.

2. Hundreds of people _____crowded_____ into the tiny space.

3. She ran _____around_____ the track.

4. Cover your eyes and _____count_____ to ten.

▶ **Write the Spelling Word that best completes each group.**

5. yelled, screamed, _____shouted_____

6. quiet, noisy, _____loud_____

7. water, drink, _____fountain_____

8. cabin, hut, _____house_____

9. noise, voice, _____sound_____

10. hop, jump, _____bounce_____

11. north, east, _____south_____

▶ **Write the following Spelling Words:** *however, howl, growl,* and *crown.* **Use your best handwriting.**

12. _____however_____   14. _____growl_____

13. _____howl_____   15. _____crown_____

SPELLING WORDS

1. crown
2. proud
3. however
4. count
5. crowded
6. around
7. south
8. loud
9. house
10. shouted
11. howl
12. growl
13. bounce
14. fountain
15. sound

Handwriting Tip: Make sure a *w* does not look like a *v*.

_____

- - - - - - - -
W
_____

Harcourt

SPELLING WORDS

1. crown
2. proud
3. however
4. count
5. crowded
6. around
7. south
8. loud
9. house
10. shouted
11. howl
12. growl
13. bounce
14. fountain
15. sound

SPELLING STRATEGY

Placeholder Spelling

When you are not sure how to spell a word, write the word the way it sounds, and circle it. Then look up the correct spelling in a dictionary before you write the final draft.

▶ **Circle six words that do not look right. Check the spelling. Then write the misspelled words correctly.** Responses may be given in any order.

bounce   (croun)   (sownd)

(showted)   howl   (fowntain)

(sowth)   (howse)   growl

1. _____crown_____   4. _____fountain_____

2. _____sound_____   5. _____south_____

3. _____shouted_____   6. _____house_____

▶ **Read the poster. Circle six words that do not look right. Then write the misspelled words correctly.**

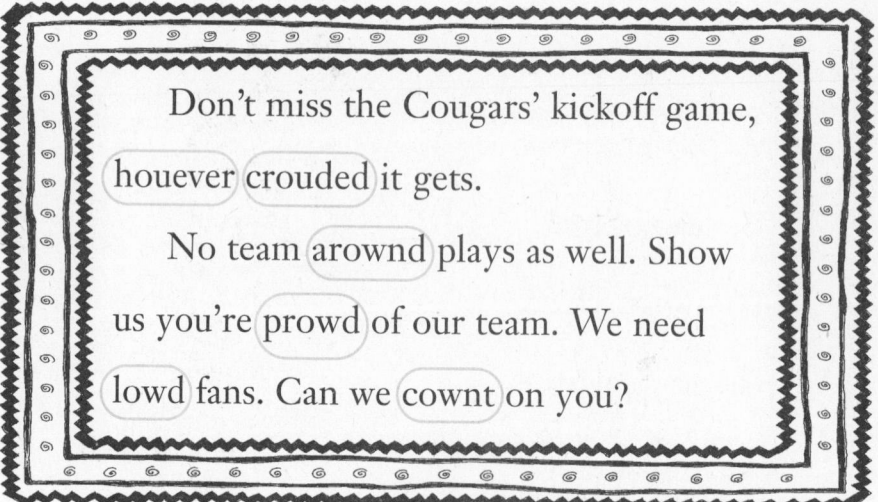

Don't miss the Cougars' kickoff game, (houever) (crouded) it gets.

No team (arownd) plays as well. Show us you're (prowd) of our team. We need (lowd) fans. Can we (cownt) on you?

7. _____however_____   10. _____proud_____

8. _____crowded_____   11. _____loud_____

9. _____around_____   12. _____count_____

Harcourt

Name _____

▶ **Word Puzzle** Write Spelling Words to complete this puzzle. Use the letters to help you.

6.
p

3. a r o u n d

5. s o

4. h u o

2. c r o w d e d

r u

1. s o u t h

w e

n d

SPELLING WORDS

1. crown
2. proud
3. however
4. count
5. crowded
6. around
7. south
8. loud
9. house
10. shouted
11. howl
12. growl
13. bounce
14. fountain
15. sound

▶ **Smaller Words** Write the Spelling Words that have these smaller words in them.

7. begins with <u>grow</u>   growl

8. ends with <u>ever</u>   however

9. begins with <u>crow</u>   crowded or crown

10. ends with <u>ounce</u>   bounce

11. ends with <u>owl</u>   howl or growl

12. ends with <u>in</u>   fountain

Harcourt

Practice Test

▶ **Read each sentence. Decide if the spelling of the underlined word is correct or incorrect. Fill in the oval next to the correct answer.**

1. My brother <u>knocked</u> on the door three times.

    ⬭ correct   ⬭ incorrect

2. We saw a train <u>reck</u> on television.

    ⬭ correct   ⬭ incorrect

3. Our planet is a <u>sphere</u>.

    ⬭ correct   ⬭ incorrect

4. We used <u>ruff</u> sandpaper on the wood.

    ⬭ correct   ⬭ incorrect

5. The letter was <u>written</u> in code.

    ⬭ correct   ⬭ incorrect

6. He is <u>nowne</u> for his funny jokes.

    ⬭ correct   ⬭ incorrect

7. Jan <u>chot</u> a perfect basket to win the game.

    ⬭ correct   ⬭ incorrect

8. Do your socks <u>match</u>?

    ⬭ correct   ⬭ incorrect

9. They did not have <u>enough</u> time to finish.

    ⬭ correct   ⬭ incorrect

10. I jumped when I heard the <u>crash</u> of lightning.

    ⬭ correct   ⬭ incorrect

Harcourt

Name _____

▶ **Read each sentence. Fill in the oval next to the correctly spelled word that completes each sentence.**

1. Would you like to travel into outer _____?

   ⬭ space   ⬭ spas   ⬭ spase

2. He used a _____ to draw the rocket.

   ⬭ pensil   ⬭ pencel   ⬭ pencil

3. Where is the _____ station?

   ⬭ polise   ⬭ police   ⬭ poleece

4. We saw _____ waves on the ocean.

   ⬭ huje   ⬭ huege   ⬭ huge

5. A strong wind can _____ small boats.

   ⬭ destroy   ⬭ destroi   ⬭ distroy

6. Ted was _____ on his birthday.

   ⬭ joiyful   ⬭ joiful   ⬭ joyful

7. Don't _____ the surprise!

   ⬭ spoil   ⬭ spoyl   ⬭ spiol

8. The new company will _____ fifty people.

   ⬭ imploy   ⬭ emploi   ⬭ employ

9. She is _____ to her family and friends.

   ⬭ loyal   ⬭ loiyl   ⬭ loil

10. Please lower your _____.

    ⬭ voyce   ⬭ vois   ⬭ voice

Harcourt

SPELLING WORDS

1. brother's
2. brothers
3. uncle's
4. uncles
5. sister's
6. sisters
7. sisters'
8. man's
9. men's
10. child's
11. girls
12. girl's
13. girls'
14. mine
15. yours

Handwriting Tip: Be careful not to close up the space when writing an *s*.

Possessives and Plurals

▶ Write the Spelling Word that best completes each pair of sentences.

1. The shoes belong to the girls.

   They are the _____girls'_____ shoes.

2. The toy belongs to the child.

   It is the _____child's_____ toy.

3. The book belongs to my uncle.

   It is my _____uncle's_____ book.

4. The hat belongs to the man.

   It is the _____man's_____ hat.

5. This pen belongs to you.

   This pen is _____yours_____.

6. The dresses belong to the sisters.

   These are the _____sisters'_____ dresses.

▶ Put these words in alphabetical order.

   sisters   girls   uncles   mine   brothers

   7. _____brothers_____   10. _____sisters_____

   8. _____girls_____   11. _____uncles_____

   9. _____mine_____

▶ Write the following Spelling Words: *brother's, sister's, men's,* and *girl's.* Use your best handwriting.

   12. _____brother's_____   14. _____men's_____

   13. _____sister's_____   15. _____girl's_____

SPELLING PRACTICE BOOK

LESSON 11

Harcourt

Name _____

▶ **Choose the word that correctly completes each sentence. Write the word on the line.**

1. Ellie wore her (**sister's, sisters**) dress.

   _____ sister's _____

2. We are looking for my (**brother's,**

   brothers) mitt. _____ brother's _____

3. The (**mens, men's**) choir sang in the

   evening. _____ men's _____

4. He forgot a snack, so I gave him some of

   (**mines, mine**). _____ mine _____

5. Is this blue sweater (**yours, your's**)?

   _____ yours _____

▶ **Add s, 's, or ' to each numbered word to make a Spelling Word. Then write the word.**

> Come to our family party. The **(6)** (uncle) will make the cakes and pies. All of the **(7)** (brother) will bring hot dogs. The **(8)** (girl) will bring juice. We can all ride to the picnic grounds in my three **(9)** (sisters) cars.

6. _____ uncles _____   8. _____ girls _____

7. _____ brothers _____   9. _____ sisters' _____

SPELLING WORDS

1. brother's
2. brothers
3. uncle's
4. uncles
5. sister's
6. sisters
7. sisters'
8. man's
9. men's
10. child's
11. girls
12. girl's
13. girls'
14. mine
15. yours

SPELLING STRATEGY

Plurals and Possessives Rules

Add *s* to a word to make it mean more than one (plural). To show ownership (possessive), add an apostrophe or an apostrophe and an *s*.

Harcourt

SPELLING WORDS

1. brother's
2. brothers
3. uncle's
4. uncles
5. sister's
6. sisters
7. sisters'
8. man's
9. men's
10. child's
11. girls
12. girl's
13. girls'
14. mine
15. yours

▶ **Picture Clues** Write the Spelling Word that matches each picture.

1.  _sisters or girls_

2. aunts and  _uncles_

3.  _brothers_

4.  _sister's or girl's_ book

▶ **Complete the Phrase** Read each phrase and the two answer choices. Write the correct Spelling Word on the line.

5. two (**sister's, sisters'**) bicycles _sisters'_

6. one (**man's, men's**) job _man's_

7. my (**uncle's, uncles**) shoe _uncle's_

8. one (**girls, girl's**) room _girl's_

9. four (**girls, girls'**) parents _girls'_

10. one (**childs, child's**) friend _child's_

Harcourt

Name _____

Words with /ô/

▶ Write Spelling Words from the box to complete the story.

| taught | song | because | pause | crawl |

We had a family talent show. My baby brother had just learned to **(1)** ___crawl___, so he did that. My sister sang a **(2)** ___song___. Dad had **(3)** ___taught___ me the drums, but I had to **(4)** ___pause___ in the middle of my act. My mom clapped loudly **(5)** ___because___, she said, everyone was great.

▶ Write a Spelling Word for each clue.

6. sunrise ___dawn___

7. rhymes with *dawn* ___lawn___

8. rule ___law___

9. a kind of bird ___hawk___

10. writer ___author___

11. clothes that need to be washed ___laundry___

▶ Write the following Spelling Words: *soft, lost, long,* and *frost.* Use your best handwriting.

12. ___soft___   **14.** ___long___

13. ___lost___   **15.** ___frost___

SPELLING WORDS

1. song
2. law
3. because
4. soft
5. dawn
6. crawl
7. lost
8. taught
9. long
10. pause
11. frost
12. lawn
13. hawk
14. laundry
15. author

Handwriting Tip: Make sure your *o*s do not look like *a*s.

_____

O

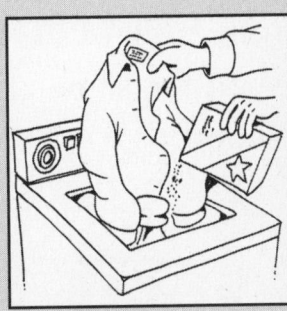

SPELLING WORDS

1. song
2. law
3. because
4. soft
5. dawn
6. crawl
7. lost
8. taught
9. long
10. pause
11. frost
12. lawn
13. hawk
14. laundry
15. author

SPELLING STRATEGY

Sounds and Letters

If a word does not look right, say the word. Listen for the vowel sound. Think of other letters that can spell the same sound.

▶ **What's wrong with each word in the box? Follow the directions to write the Spelling Words correctly.** Order may vary.

becuase	craul	sawng
luandry	frawst	lau

Change *au* to *aw* to correct two words.
Change *aw* to *o* to correct two words.
Reverse two letters to correct two words.

1. _____crawl_____
2. _____law_____
3. _____song_____
4. _____frost_____
5. _____because_____
6. _____laundry_____

▶ **Read the story. Circle the six misspelled words, and then write the correct spellings on the lines below.**

Lin got up before (daun.) She looked out her window and was surprised. A (hok) was sitting on her front (laun.) Lin thought the big bird looked (lawst.) She saw the bird flap its wings, turn its head toward her, and (pawse.) Then the bird flew away. "So (laung,) pretty bird," Lin whispered.

7. _____dawn_____
8. _____hawk_____
9. _____lawn_____
10. _____lost_____
11. _____pause_____
12. _____long_____

SPELLING PRACTICE BOOK

LESSON 12

Harcourt

Name _____

▶ **Use the Clues** Write a Spelling Word for each clue.

1. This word tells how a baby's blanket feels.

    _____soft_____

2. This word is the opposite of

    short. ____long____

3. This word names something you do with

    your hands and knees. ____crawl____

4. This word goes with *lose* and *losing.*

    _____lost_____

5. This word names someone who writes.

    ____author____

6. This word names a place where

    grass grows. ____lawn____

7. This word goes with *teach* and *teaching.*

    ____taught____

▶ **Rhyme Time** On each line, write a Spelling Word that rhymes with the underlined words.

8. Is it <u>wrong</u> to sing a <u>long</u> ____song____?

9. I saw a <u>fawn</u> on the <u>lawn</u> at ____dawn____.

10. The couch in the <u>loft</u> of Mr. <u>Croft</u> is

    ____soft____.

11. A judge <u>saw</u> a <u>flaw</u> in the new ____law____.

12. Don't <u>gawk</u> at the ____hawk____, or it will

    <u>squawk</u>.

SPELLING WORDS

1. song
2. law
3. because
4. soft
5. dawn
6. crawl
7. lost
8. taught
9. long
10. pause
11. frost
12. lawn
13. hawk
14. laundry
15. author

Harcourt

SPELLING WORDS

1. boots
2. grouped
3. shook
4. school
5. looked
6. hood
7. choose
8. brook
9. zoomed
10. balloon
11. loose
12. soot
13. understood
14. cartoon
15. afternoon

Handwriting Tip: Be sure to space your letters properly.

soot

Words with /o͞o/ and /o͝o/

▶ Write the Spelling Word that matches each picture.

1. _____ hood _____

2. _____ boots _____

3. _____ balloon _____

4. _____ school _____

▶ Write the Spelling Words that mean the same or nearly the same as the given words.

5. comic   _____ cartoon _____

6. stream   _____ brook _____

7. baggy   _____ loose _____

8. knew   _____ understood _____

9. glanced   _____ looked _____

10. shivered   _____ shook _____

11. pick   _____ choose _____

▶ Write the following Spelling Words: *grouped, zoomed, soot,* and *afternoon.* Use your best handwriting.

12. _____ grouped _____   14. _____ soot _____

13. _____ zoomed _____   15. _____ afternoon _____

Harcourt

Name_____

▶ **Write a Spelling Word that rhymes.**

1. boomed   _zoomed_

2. foot   _soot_

3. roots   _boots_

4. pool   _school_

5. cooked   _looked_

6. goose   _loose_

▶ **Write the Spelling Word that is correct.**

7. We **(grouped, grooped)** the children by threes for our field trip. _grouped_

8. There is a **(brook, brouk)** behind our house. _brook_

9. I have soccer practice this **(afternoun, afternoon)**. _afternoon_

10. Wear the jacket with the **(hood, houd)**. _hood_

11. No one **(understoud, understood)** the question. _understood_

12. What is your favorite **(cartune, cartoon)**? _cartoon_

SPELLING WORDS

1. boots
2. grouped
3. shook
4. school
5. looked
6. hood
7. choose
8. brook
9. zoomed
10. balloon
11. loose
12. soot
13. understood
14. cartoon
15. afternoon

SPELLING STRATEGY

Rhyming Words

If you are unsure how to spell a word, think of a rhyming word that you know how to spell. Try that ending.

SPELLING WORDS

1. boots
2. grouped
3. shook
4. school
5. looked
6. hood
7. choose
8. brook
9. zoomed
10. balloon
11. loose
12. soot
13. understood
14. cartoon
15. afternoon

▶ **Categories** Read the label on each balloon. Write the Spelling Words that belong on that balloon. Responses within categories may be given in any order.

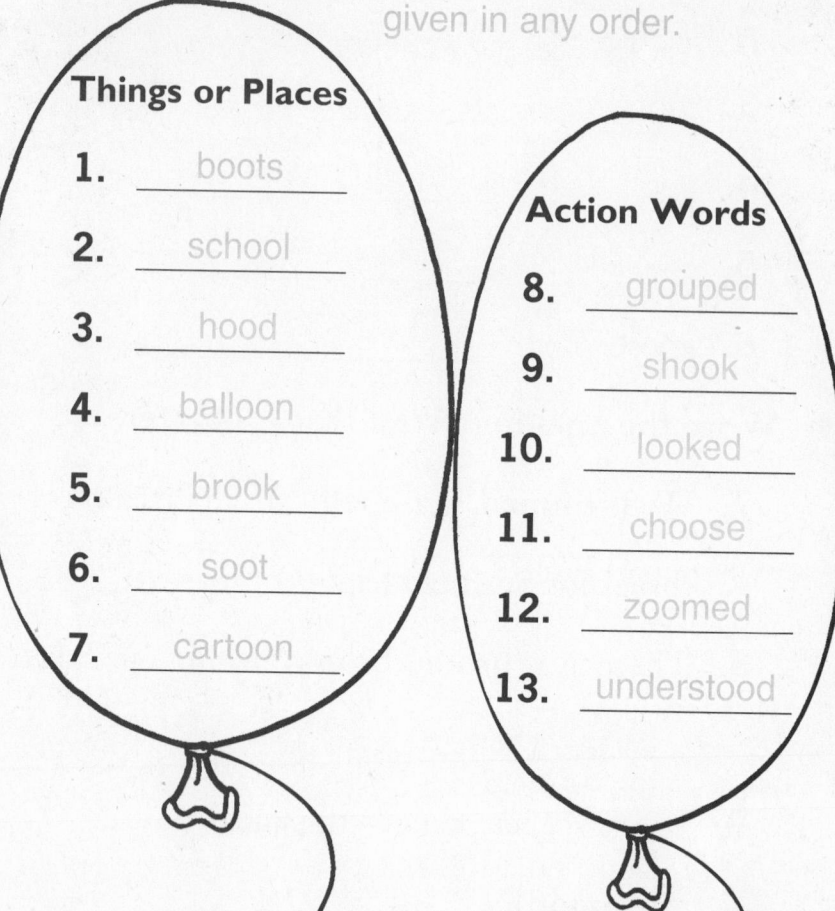

Things or Places

1. ___boots___
2. ___school___
3. ___hood___
4. ___balloon___
5. ___brook___
6. ___soot___
7. ___cartoon___

Action Words

8. ___grouped___
9. ___shook___
10. ___looked___
11. ___choose___
12. ___zoomed___
13. ___understood___

▶ **Use the Clues** Write a Spelling Word for each clue.

14. I am often carried by a clown. Pop me and I will come down. ___balloon___

15. When it rains, you wear these on your feet. With a raincoat your outfit is complete.

    ___boots___

SPELLING PRACTICE BOOK

LESSON 13

Harcourt

Name _____

Words with /är/

SPELLING WORDS

1. started
2. card
3. park
4. smart
5. star
6. shark
7. mark
8. barber
9. party
10. pardon
11. bark
12. tart
13. carpet
14. farther
15. barn

▶ **Write a Spelling Word for each clue.**

1. a large fish with sharp teeth ___shark___

2. began ___started___

3. the sound a dog makes ___bark___

4. an event where people gather to have fun ___party___

5. able to think quickly ___smart___

6. forgive ___pardon___

▶ **Write the Spelling Word that could take the place of each group of words.**

7. floor covering ___carpet___

8. shining object in the sky ___star___

9. place where farm animals are kept ___barn___

10. grassy place with trees ___park___

11. small flaky crust with fruit filling ___tart___

▶ **Write the following Spelling Words: *card*, *mark*, *barber*, and *farther*. Use your best handwriting.**

12. ___card___   14. ___barber___

13. ___mark___   15. ___farther___

Handwriting Tip: Be sure your letters sit evenly on the bottom line.

star

Harcourt

SPELLING WORDS

1. started
2. card
3. park
4. smart
5. star
6. shark
7. mark
8. barber
9. party
10. pardon
11. bark
12. tart
13. carpet
14. farther
15. barn

▶ **Say aloud each word below. Circle and write the word in each row that is spelled correctly.**

1. (barn)   baurn   barne   _____barn_____

2. pordon   (pardon)   pahdon   _____pardon_____

3. parke   paurk   (park)   _____park_____

4. frather   (farther)   fahther   _____farther_____

5. (started)   strated   staurted   _____started_____

6. barke   baurk   (bark)   _____bark_____

▶ **Read the invitation. Circle the six misspelled words. Then write the correct spellings on the lines below.**

Dear Mom and Dad,

You are invited to a (paurty) in our classroom. We will show you our reports on the tiger (shrak.) You will see how (smaurt) we are. We will put on a play about a lost (staur.) Please (maurk) this day on a (carde:) Monday, at 7 P.M.

7. _____party_____   10. _____star_____

8. _____shark_____   11. _____mark_____

9. _____smart_____   12. _____card_____

SPELLING STRATEGY

Careful Pronunciation

When you are proofreading and are not sure of the spelling of a word, say the word aloud. Think about the letters that usually make those sounds.

Harcourt

Name _____

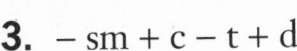

▶ **Word Ladders** Make a Spelling Word for each rung of the ladder by changing letters as directed. Start at the bottom of each ladder.

SPELLING WORDS

1. started
2. card
3. park
4. smart
5. star
6. shark
7. mark
8. barber
9. party
10. pardon
11. bark
12. tart
13. carpet
14. farther
15. barn

3. − sm + c − t + d

2. − p + sm − y

1. − k + ty

Start here

card

smart

party

park

6. + ted

5. − sh + st − k

4. − m + sh

Start here

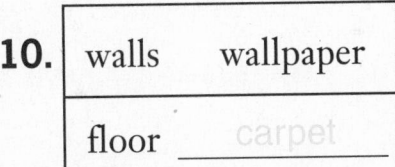

started

star

shark

mark

▶ **Word Groups** Write the Spelling Word that best fits with each group of words below.

7.	pie	cookie
	cake	tart

10.	walls	wallpaper
	floor	carpet

8.	close	closer
	far	farther

11.	chair	scissors
	hair	barber

9.	meow	quack
	moo	bark

12.	people	house
	horses	barn

Harcourt

SPELLING WORDS

1. bear
2. tear
3. haircut
4. stairs
5. wear
6. airplane
7. compare
8. repair
9. pear
10. prepare
11. stare
12. glare
13. sharing
14. fairy
15. aware

Handwriting Tip: Close the letter *a* so that it does not look like the letter *u*.

Words with /âr/

▶ **Write a Spelling Word to complete each sentence.**

1. I went to the barber to get a _____ haircut _____.

2. The pilot flies an _____ airplane _____.

3. A _____ pear _____ is a fruit.

4. She will _____ wear _____ her new sweater.

5. Cinderella had a _____ fairy _____ godmother.

6. We went to another store to _____ compare _____ prices.

▶ **Write a Spelling Word for each clue.**

7. This is another word for *fix*.   repair

8. a large animal that growls   bear

9. These are a set of steps.   stairs

10. You are this when you know what is going on around you.   aware

11. This is a rip in a piece of cloth.   tear

▶ **Write the following Spelling Words:** *glare, prepare, stare,* **and** *sharing.* **Use your best handwriting.**

12. _____ glare _____   14. _____ stare _____

13. _____ prepare _____   15. _____ sharing _____

SPELLING PRACTICE BOOK

LESSON 15

Harcourt

Name _____

▶ **Proofread each sentence backward (from right to left). Circle the two errors in each sentence. Then write the Spelling Words correctly.**

1–2. Please be (awair) of the (tair) in my coat.

3–4. What should we (wair) on the (airplan)?

5–6. How would you (compair) an elf and a (fary)?

1. _____aware_____   4. _____airplane_____

2. _____tear_____   5. _____compare_____

3. _____wear_____   6. _____fairy_____

▶ **Read the story. Circle the six misspelled words. Then write the correct spellings.**

The Three Bears Come Home

Mama Bear looked at the three empty bowls. "I don't mind (shaering)," she said, "but this isn't fair." Then the three bears went up the (stears) and found Goldilocks. "Look who's sleeping in my bed!" cried the baby (baer). Goldilocks woke up and screamed. "Hush," said Mama Bear. "We won't hurt you. Don't (stayre) at me. Help me (prepair) some more porridge. Then help Daddy Bear (repear) the chair you broke. Then you can go home."

---

7. _____sharing_____   10. _____stare_____

8. _____stairs_____   11. _____prepare_____

9. _____bear_____   12. _____repair_____

SPELLING WORDS
1. bear
2. tear
3. haircut
4. stairs
5. wear
6. airplane
7. compare
8. repair
9. pear
10. prepare
11. stare
12. glare
13. sharing
14. fairy
15. aware

SPELLING STRATEGY

Reading Backward

When you proofread, try reading backward to spot errors. Start with the last word and end with the first.

Harcourt

Name _____

SPELLING WORDS

1. bear
2. tear
3. haircut
4. stairs
5. wear
6. airplane
7. compare
8. repair
9. pear
10. prepare
11. stare
12. glare
13. sharing
14. fairy
15. aware

▶ **Label the Pictures** Write Spelling Words that finish each sentence and tell about each picture.

A **(1)** _____ bear _____

holds a **(2)** _____ pear _____ .

I **(3)** _____ prepare _____

to give the boy a **(4)** _____ haircut _____ .

I can't **(5)** _____ wear _____ this shirt.

It has a **(6)** _____ tear _____ .

▶ **Word Shapes** Write a Spelling Word in each word shape.

7. | s | h | a | r | i | n | g |

8. | g | l | a | r | e |

Harcourt

SPELLING PRACTICE BOOK

LESSON 15

Practice Test

▶ **Read the sentence. Find the underlined word that is spelled correctly. Fill in the oval next to the correct spelling.**

1. My <u>sisters</u> chair is next to <u>mine</u>.

   ⊂⊃ sisters   ⊂⊃ mine

2. The dog in the <u>cartoun</u> <u>zoomed</u> across the screen.

   ⊂⊃ cartoun   ⊂⊃ zoomed

3. We watched the <u>balloon</u> float over the <u>brooke</u>.

   ⊂⊃ balloon   ⊂⊃ brooke

4. Don't <u>stayre</u> at his bad <u>haircut</u>.

   ⊂⊃ stayre   ⊂⊃ haircut

5. The dog <u>started</u> to <u>bahrk</u> when we drove away.

   ⊂⊃ started   ⊂⊃ bahrk

6. Do you know a <u>long</u> <u>sawng</u> we can sing?

   ⊂⊃ long   ⊂⊃ sawng

7. The <u>awthor</u> wrote about the new <u>law</u>.

   ⊂⊃ awthor   ⊂⊃ law

8. Dad <u>taught</u> me how to do the <u>lawndry</u>.

   ⊂⊃ taught   ⊂⊃ lawndry

9. The <u>frawst</u> on the <u>lawn</u> sparkled in the sun.

   ⊂⊃ frawst   ⊂⊃ lawn

10. I am late <u>because</u> I got <u>laust</u>.

    ⊂⊃ because   ⊂⊃ laust

11. He <u>shouk</u> the <u>soot</u> from his clothes.

    ⊂⊃ shouk   ⊂⊃ soot

Harcourt

Name _____

▶ **Read each group of words. Find the word in each group that is spelled correctly. Fill in the circle next to that word.**

1 (A) looce
   (B) loose
   (C) losse
   (D) loos

2 (F) grooped
   (G) grewped
   (H) grouped
   (J) groupt

3 (A) hud
   (B) hood
   (C) hude
   (D) hoode

4 (F) staire
   (G) stawr
   (H) starr
   (J) star

5 (A) barn
   (B) barne
   (C) bairn
   (D) bahrn

6 (F) airplain
   (G) airplane
   (H) areplane
   (J) airplain

7 (A) shark
   (B) sharke
   (C) shrak
   (D) shork

8 (F) baer
   (G) bear
   (H) beare
   (J) bair

9 (A) awair
   (B) awear
   (C) awar
   (D) aware

10 (F) repayre
   (G) repare
   (H) repair
   (J) repear

11 (A) farther
   (B) forther
   (C) ferther
   (D) faerther

12 (F) barbar
   (G) bareber
   (H) bahber
   (J) barber

Harcourt

REVIEW

Name _____

Words with /ôr/

▶ **Write Spelling Words to complete the story.**

I like to get up early in the **(1)** __morning__

to ride my **(2)** __horse__ . I can't ride when it

rains. Today was the **(3)** __fourth__ rainy day

in a row. Another big rain **(4)** __storm__ is

coming tomorrow.

▶ **Write a Spelling Word for each clue.**

5. a harbor _____ port

6. to tell _____ warn

7. woods _____ forest

8. used _____ worn

9. utensils _____ forks

10. a battle _____ war

11. flowed _____ poured

▶ **Write the following Spelling Words:** *porch,*
form, court, **and** *important.* **Use your best**
handwriting.

12. _____ porch

13. _____ form

14. _____ court

15. _____ important

1. *forks*
2. *worn*
3. *form*
4. *fourth*
5. *war*
6. *storm*
7. *horse*
8. *warn*
9. *morning*
10. *forest*
11. *court*
12. *porch*
13. *poured*
14. *port*
15. *important*

Handwriting Tip: Be sure to space letters properly so they are easy to read.

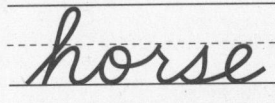

SPELLING WORDS

1. forks
2. worn
3. form
4. fourth
5. war
6. storm
7. horse
8. warn
9. morning
10. forest
11. court
12. porch
13. poured
14. port
15. important

SPELLING STRATEGY

Comparing Spellings

If a word does not look right, try writing each vowel sound with all its possible spellings. Compare the spellings. Then choose the one that looks right.

▶ **Compare the two spellings for each Spelling Word. Then write the correct spelling for each word.**

1. form *or* fourm _____ form

2. war *or* wor _____ war

3. wourn *or* worn _____ worn

4. important *or* impartant _____ important

5. poared *or* poured _____ poured

6. court *or* cort _____ court

▶ **Read the letter. Compare the two spellings in parentheses. Circle the correct spelling, and then write each Spelling Word.**

Dear Mom and Dad,

   I am having fun at Uncle Jack's farm. Every **(7)** (morning, marning) I feed the chickens. The **(8)** (farth, fourth) day I was here, I helped milk the cows. I rode a big **(9)** (harse, horse) all by myself. We play tennis on the tennis **(10)** (court, cort). One day I watched a **(11)** (storm, starm) from the **(12)** (pourch, porch).

             Love,
             Sam

7. _____ morning   10. _____ court

8. _____ fourth   11. _____ storm

9. _____ horse   12. _____ porch

Harcourt

Name _____

▶ **A Cartoon** Circle the four misspelled words in the cartoon. Then write the words correctly.

"I wourn you! The sky is going to fall!" said the rooster.

"No, it's not. It's just a sturm!" said the hourse. Then it poored.

1. _____warn_____   3. _____horse_____

2. _____storm_____   4. _____poured_____

▶ **What Am I?** Write the Spelling Word that answers each riddle.

5. I am a place for ships. _____port_____

6. I am a place where many trees grow. _____forest_____

7. I am an outside part of a house. _____porch_____

8. We are used to pick up food. _____forks_____

9. I am the early part of the day. _____morning_____

10. I am the opposite of peace. _____war_____

SPELLING WORDS

1. forks
2. worn
3. form
4. fourth
5. war
6. storm
7. horse
8. warn
9. morning
10. forest
11. court
12. porch
13. poured
14. port
15. important

Harcourt

SPELLING WORDS

1. hear
2. one
3. won
4. way
5. heard
6. flower
7. our
8. flour
9. weigh
10. here
11. beat
12. herd
13. beet
14. hair
15. hare

Handwriting Tip: Be sure that each letter you write is the correct size. Tall letters touch both the top and bottom lines.

weigh

Homophones

▶ **Write a Spelling Word to complete each sentence.**

1. How much do the apples _____weigh_____?

2. I _____heard_____ you call my name.

3. A _____beet_____ is a purple vegetable.

4. Two plus _____one_____ equals three.

5. Ask your mom if you can play at _____our_____ house.

6. Tasha _____won_____ the race.

7. Which _____way_____ should we go?

8. The _____hare_____ had long ears.

9. He has brown _____hair_____.

10. A rose is a _____flower_____.

11. Add _____flour_____ to the cake batter.

▶ **Write the following Spelling Words: *hear*, *here*, *beat*, and *herd*. Use your best handwriting.**

12. _____hear_____

13. _____here_____

14. _____beat_____

15. _____herd_____

SPELLING PRACTICE BOOK

LESSON 17

Harcourt

Name _____

► **Use the homophones in parentheses to complete each sentence.**

1. ___One___ day, Flo ___won___ the race. (won, one)

2. The ___hare___ has soft ___hair___. (hare, hair)

3. I ___heard___ the mooing of a ___herd___ of cows. (herd, heard)

4. A ___way___ to measure sugar is to ___weigh___ it. (weigh, way)

5. You can ___hear___ better over ___here___.

► **Circle the Spelling Word that makes sense in each sentence. Then write the word.**

6. I put a (**flower**, flour) in a vase. ___flower___

7. I need (flower, **flour**), sugar, and eggs to make cookies. ___flour___

8. Lena (beet, **beat**) me to the finish line. ___beat___

9. We (herd, **heard**) the good news on the radio. ___heard___

10. Please show me the right (weigh, **way**) to do this. ___way___

SPELLING WORDS

1. hear
2. one
3. won
4. way
5. heard
6. flower
7. our
8. flour
9. weigh
10. here
11. beat
12. herd
13. beet
14. hair
15. hare

SPELLING STRATEGY

Homophones

When you write a word that has a homophone, think about the spellings and meanings of both words. Choose the spelling of the word that makes sense in the sentence.

Harcourt

SPELLING WORDS

1. hear
2. one
3. won
4. way
5. heard
6. flower
7. our
8. flour
9. weigh
10. here
11. beat
12. herd
13. beet
14. hair
15. hare

▶ **Rhyme Time** On each line, write a Spelling Word that rhymes with the underlined word.

1. At what <u>hour</u> will ____our____ train arrive?

2. I walked down ____here____ from somewhere <u>near</u>.

3. The princess tossed a pretty pink ____flower____ from the top of the <u>tower</u>.

4. She runs well in the <u>heat</u> and is hard to ____beat____.

▶ **Crossword Puzzle** Write Spelling Words to complete this puzzle. Use the clues to help you.

ACROSS

5. you use a scale to do this
6. a number less than two
7. rhymes with *day*
8. a large group of animals

DOWN

9. the team ____ the game
10. used your ears
11. a purple vegetable

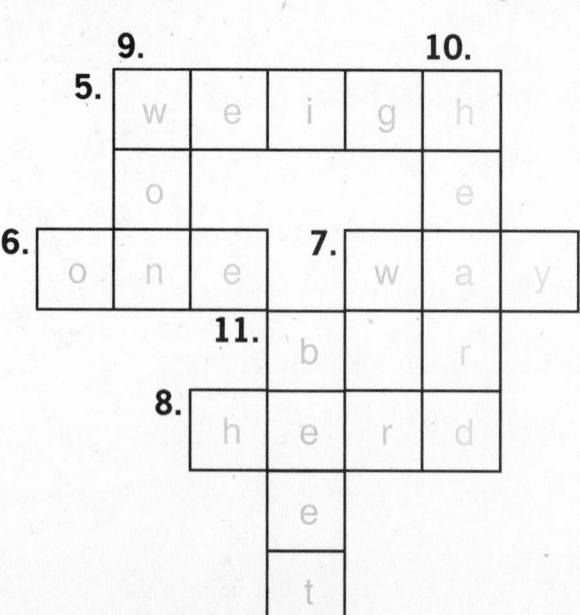

SPELLING PRACTICE BOOK

LESSON 17

Harcourt

Name _____

Words with /ûr/

▶ Write the Spelling Word that best matches each mini-definition.

SPELLING WORDS

1. curl
2. birth
3. burned
4. perfect
5. thirty
6. church
7. firm
8. skirt
9. clerk
10. jerked
11. dirt
12. shirt
13. person
14. purse
15. term

1. overcooked _____burned_____

2. flawless _____perfect_____

3. a piece of clothing with sleeves _____shirt_____

4. number after twenty-nine _____thirty_____

5. a human _____person_____

▶ Put these words in alphabetical order.

curl	firm	skirt
jerked	purse	term

6. _____curl_____   9. _____purse_____

7. _____firm_____   10. _____skirt_____

8. _____jerked_____   11. _____term_____

▶ Write the following Spelling Words: *birth*, *church*, *clerk*, and *dirt*. Use your best handwriting.

12. _____birth_____   14. _____clerk_____

13. _____church_____   15. _____dirt_____

Handwriting Tip: Be sure that the upward curve of the *r* stroke continues from the end stroke of an *i*, an *e*, and a *u*. Make sure that it is followed by a short downward curve, and then by a longer downward curve.

her

Harcourt

SPELLING WORDS

1. curl
2. birth
3. burned
4. perfect
5. thirty
6. church
7. firm
8. skirt
9. clerk
10. jerked
11. dirt
12. shirt
13. person
14. purse
15. term

SPELLING STRATEGY

Placeholder Spelling

If you are not sure how to spell a vowel sound in a word, try different spellings for that sound. Choose the one that looks right, and then check the spelling in a dictionary.

▶ **Read each sentence. Add *ir, er,* or *ur* to complete the Spelling Word. Check it with the Spelling Word list. Then write each word correctly.**

1. My dog gave b__i__ __r__th to five puppies.
   _____birth_____

2. We b__u__ __r__ned two logs. _____burned_____

3. Nobody is p__e__ __r__fect. _____perfect_____

4. My cat likes to c__u__ __r__l up on the bed.
   _____curl_____

5. The store cl__e__ __r__k handed me my
   change. _____clerk_____

▶ **Read the story. Circle the five misspelled words. Then write the correct spellings on the lines below.**

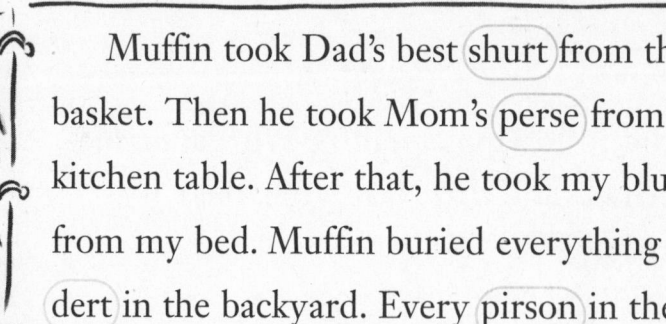

Muffin took Dad's best (shurt) from the laundry basket. Then he took Mom's (perse) from the kitchen table. After that, he took my blue (skert) from my bed. Muffin buried everything in the (dert) in the backyard. Every (pirson) in the house was missing something.

6. _____shirt_____   9. _____dirt_____

7. _____purse_____   10. _____person_____

8. _____skirt_____

Harcourt

Name_____

▶ **Unscramble the Words** Rearrange each group of letters to write a Spelling Word. Hint: Look for *er, ur,* or *ir,* and write those letters together.

1. thirb   birth
2. seonrp   person
3. kejred   jerked
4. tefeprc   perfect
5. metr   term
6. rifm   firm

▶ **Picture Clues** Write the Spelling Word that matches each picture. Circle the letters that make the /ûr/ sound.

7. ___church___

10. ___thirty___

8. ___burned___

11. ___shirt___

9. ___skirt___

12. ___purse___

SPELLING WORDS
1. curl
2. birth
3. burned
4. perfect
5. thirty
6. church
7. firm
8. skirt
9. clerk
10. jerked
11. dirt
12. shirt
13. person
14. purse
15. term

Harcourt

SPELLING WORDS

1. pulled
2. begged
3. hugged
4. silly
5. correct
6. latter
7. matter
8. supper
9. common
10. lesson
11. collect
12. setting
13. bottles
14. different
15. jelly

Handwriting Tip: Be sure that your writing is neat and easy to read. Slant all the letters in the same direction.

Words with Double Consonants

▶ Write the Spelling Words that mean the same or nearly the same as the given words.

1. right _____ correct

2. dinner _____ supper

3. to gather _____ collect

4. funny _____ silly

5. unlike _____ different

6. tugged _____ pulled

7. squeezed _____ hugged

▶ Write the Spelling Word that matches each clue.

8. where a story takes place _____ setting

9. things that hold milk and water _____ bottles

10. something you learn _____ lesson

11. asked for again and again _____ begged

▶ Write the following Spelling Words: *latter, matter, common,* and *jelly.* Use your best handwriting.

12. _____ latter   14. _____ common

13. _____ matter   15. _____ jelly

Harcourt

Name_____

▶ Say aloud each word below. Circle the word in each pair that is spelled correctly. Then write the word.

1. (bottles)   botles   _bottles_

2. corect   (correct)   _correct_

3. sopper   (supper)   _supper_

4. commin   (common)   _common_

5. (collect)   colect   _collect_

▶ Read the book report. Circle the seven misspelled words. Then write the correct spellings on the lines below.

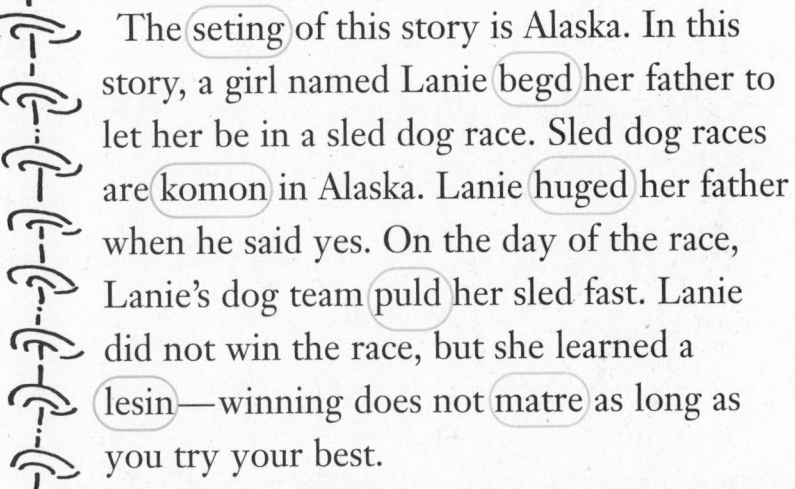

The (seting) of this story is Alaska. In this story, a girl named Lanie (begd) her father to let her be in a sled dog race. Sled dog races are (komon) in Alaska. Lanie (huged) her father when he said yes. On the day of the race, Lanie's dog team (puld) her sled fast. Lanie did not win the race, but she learned a (lesin)—winning does not (matre) as long as you try your best.

6. _setting_   10. _pulled_

7. _begged_   11. _lesson_

8. _common_   12. _matter_

9. _hugged_

SPELLING WORDS

1. pulled
2. begged
3. hugged
4. silly
5. correct
6. latter
7. matter
8. supper
9. common
10. lesson
11. collect
12. setting
13. bottles
14. different
15. jelly

S P E L L I N G
STRATEGY
Listening

Before you spell a word with double consonants in the middle, say the word aloud. Words with short vowel sounds in the first syllable are often spelled with double consonants.

1. pulled
2. begged
3. hugged
4. silly
5. correct
6. latter
7. matter
8. supper
9. common
10. lesson
11. collect
12. setting
13. bottles
14. different
15. jelly

Name _____

▶ **Sounds and Syllables** Find the Spelling Words that have each sound in the first syllable. Write the words on the lines.

Order within sets may vary.

short *a* 1. _____latter_____

2. _____matter_____

short *e* 3. _____begged_____

4. _____lesson_____

5. _____setting_____

6. _____jelly_____

short *i* 7. _____silly_____

8. _____different_____

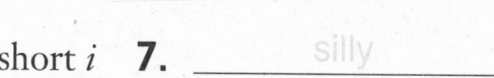

▶ **Smaller Words** Write the Spelling Words that have these smaller words in them.

9. ends with *led* _____pulled_____

10. ends with *rent* _____different_____

11. begins with *hug* _____hugged_____

▶ **Root Words** Add an ending to each root word to write a Spelling Word.

12. differ _____different_____

13. hug _____hugged_____

14. beg _____begged_____

15. pull _____pulled_____

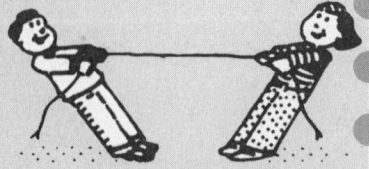

Harcourt

Name _____

Words with -er and -est

▶ **Write a Spelling Word to complete each sentence.**

1. I can run _____ faster _____ than my friend.

2. I am the _____ slowest _____ runner here.

3. This pond feels much _____ cooler _____ than the warm lake.

4. I am the _____ wildest _____ animal around. I am wilder than all the other animals in the jungle.

▶ **Write a Spelling Word for each clue.**

5. larger _____ bigger _____

6. noisier _____ louder _____

7. most unusual _____ strangest _____

8. most heat _____ hottest _____

9. thinner _____ slimmer _____

10. smartest _____ wisest _____

11. most caring _____ kindest _____

▶ **Write the following Spelling Words:** *shorter, soonest, tamer,* and *whitest.* **Use your best handwriting.**

12. _____ shorter _____   14. _____ tamer _____

13. _____ soonest _____   15. _____ whitest _____

SPELLING WORDS

1. faster
2. wisest
3. bigger
4. slowest
5. cooler
6. hottest
7. soonest
8. shorter
9. kindest
10. louder
11. slimmer
12. wildest
13. tamer
14. whitest
15. strangest

Handwriting Tip: Be sure to space the letters in a word correctly, not too close together and not too far apart.

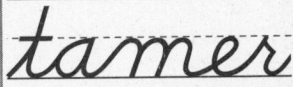

Harcourt

1. faster
2. wisest
3. bigger
4. slowest
5. cooler
6. hottest
7. soonest
8. shorter
9. kindest
10. louder
11. slimmer
12. wildest
13. tamer
14. whitest
15. strangest

SPELLING STRATEGY

Adding Endings

If a base word ends with a single consonant, ask yourself whether the vowel before the consonant is short. If it is, you need to double the final consonant before adding *-er* or *-est*.

Name_____

▶ **Add an ending from the box to write a Spelling Word.**

-er	-est

1. cool ___cooler___   4. short ___shorter___

2. soon ___soonest___   5. kind ___kindest___

3. hot ___hottest___   6. slim ___slimmer___

▶ **Read each pair of words. Circle the misspelled word. Then write the correctly spelled word on the line.**

7. (stranggest)   strangest   ___strangest___

8. whitest   (whittest)   ___whitest___

9. bigger   (biger)   ___bigger___

10. (tammer)   tamer   ___tamer___

11. (lowder)   louder   ___louder___

12. faster   (fastter)   ___faster___

▶ **Write the Spelling Word that fits in each shape.** Order may vary.

13. f a s t e r

14. l o u d e r

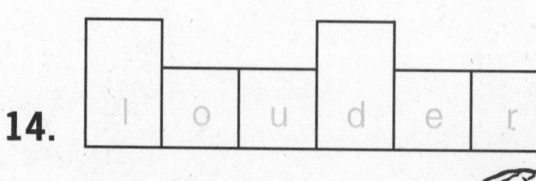

Harcourt

Name _____

▶ **Word Sets** Write the Spelling Word that completes each set of words.

1. wild, wilder, _____wildest_____

2. wise, wiser, _____wisest_____

3. slim, _____slimmer_____, slimmest

4. strange, stranger, _____strangest_____

5. cool, _____cooler_____, coolest

6. tame, _____tamer_____, tamest

▶ **Opposites** Write the Spelling Words that are the opposite of the given words.

7. coldest _____hottest_____

8. meanest _____kindest_____

9. smaller _____bigger_____

10. more quiet _____louder_____

11. taller _____shorter_____

12. fastest _____slowest_____

▶ **Unscramble the Words** Rearrange each group of letters to write a Spelling Word.

13. tiwehst _____whitest_____

14. rafest _____faster_____

15. osontes _____soonest_____

16. dtskein _____kindest_____

17. sweist _____wisest_____

SPELLING WORDS

1. faster
2. wisest
3. bigger
4. slowest
5. cooler
6. hottest
7. soonest
8. shorter
9. kindest
10. louder
11. slimmer
12. wildest
13. tamer
14. whitest
15. strangest

Harcourt

Name _____

Practice Test

▶ **Read each sentence. Fill in the oval next to the correctly spelled word that completes each sentence.**

1. I rode a _____ on my birthday.
   ⬭ hourse   ⬭ hors   ⬬ horse

2. We saw lightning during the _____.
   ⬬ storm   ⬭ stourm   ⬭ starm

3. He heard the _____ door slam.
   ⬭ poorch   ⬭ pourch   ⬬ porch

4. I have some _____ news for you.
   ⬬ important   ⬭ impourtant   ⬭ impartant

5. He eats a good breakfast every _____.
   ⬭ mourning   ⬬ morning   ⬭ moarning

6. Pedro sits in the _____ row.
   ⬬ fourth   ⬭ foarth   ⬭ forth

7. Can we bring _____ bicycles to the rally?
   ⬭ hour   ⬬ our   ⬭ are

8. Measure two cups of _____ for the cake.
   ⬬ flour   ⬭ fluor   ⬭ flower

9. She tied a blue ribbon in her long _____.
   ⬭ hare   ⬭ haer   ⬬ hair

10. I would like _____ more piece of pizza.
    ⬭ won   ⬬ one   ⬭ wone

Harcourt

REVIEW

▶ **Read each sentence. The underlined word is misspelled. Fill in the oval next to the correct spelling.**

1. She is the right <u>pirson</u> for the job.

⬭ person ⬭ purson ⬭ persin

2. We counted <u>therty</u> people on the bus.

⬭ thurty ⬭ thirtty ⬭ thirty

3. Do you have a pencil in your <u>perse</u>?

⬭ purse ⬭ purs ⬭ pirse

4. Do you like <u>silley</u> stories?

⬭ silly ⬭ sily ⬭ sillie

5. Pass the <u>jeley</u>, please!

⬭ jelley ⬭ jelly ⬭ gelly

6. Do you understand the <u>leson</u>?

⬭ lessun ⬭ lessn ⬭ lesson

7. What's the <u>mater</u> with your arm?

⬭ mattur ⬭ matter ⬭ mattar

8. We bought two <u>botles</u> of fresh orange juice.

⬭ bottles ⬭ bottels ⬭ botels

9. Pete likes to try <u>diffrent</u> foods.

⬭ diferent ⬭ difrent ⬭ different

10. Brad is <u>shortir</u> than I am.

⬭ shorter ⬭ shortr ⬭ shortur

11. What is the <u>slowist</u> animal in Africa?

⬭ slowes ⬭ slowerst ⬭ slowest

Harcourt

Name _____

Compound Words

SPELLING WORDS

1. sometimes
2. pickup
3. dishwater
4. notebook
5. upstairs
6. football
7. sunshine
8. outdoors
9. hallway
10. timeout
11. doorway
12. sunset
13. bookcase
14. everyone
15. everything

Handwriting Tip: When you write compound words, write the whole word without stopping between the two smaller words.

sun set

sunset

▶ Write a Spelling Word for each clue.

1. truck _____ pickup

2. a break in the action _____ timeout

3. a passageway _____ hallway

4. place for keeping books _____ bookcase

5. outside _____ outdoors

6. a sport _____ football

7. the second floor _____ upstairs

8. when the sun goes down _____ sunset

9. all the people _____ everyone

10. a writing pad _____ notebook

11. once in a while _____ sometimes

▶ Write the following Spelling Words: *dishwater, sunshine, doorway,* and *everything*. Use your best handwriting.

12. _____ dishwater

14. _____ doorway

13. _____ sunshine

15. _____ everything

Harcourt

Name _____

► **Circle the two words in each row that make a compound word. Then write the Spelling Word.**

1. book (dish) way (water)

   dishwater

2. (every) note (thing) water

   everything

3. way (book) (case) shine

   bookcase

4. stairs (some) ball (times)

   sometimes

5. (door) (way) dish times

   doorway

SPELLING WORDS

1. sometimes
2. pickup
3. dishwater
4. notebook
5. upstairs
6. football
7. sunshine
8. outdoors
9. hallway
10. timeout
11. doorway
12. sunset
13. bookcase
14. everyone
15. everything

► **Read the poster. Circle the six misspelled words. Then write the words correctly.**

Take a (timout) from your chores next Saturday.
Come to the school (footbal) game.
Sit in the (owtdoors).
Enjoy the bright (sunshin).
Have fun with (evryone) from school.
Pick up tickets in the school (halwaye).

SPELLING STRATEGY

Small Words

When you proofread, break compound words into two smaller words. Then check the spelling of the smaller words.

6. _timeout_   9. _sunshine_

7. _football_   10. _everyone_

8. _outdoors_   11. _hallway_

Harcourt

SPELLING WORDS

1. sometimes
2. pickup
3. dishwater
4. notebook
5. upstairs
6. football
7. sunshine
8. outdoors
9. hallway
10. timeout
11. doorway
12. sunset
13. bookcase
14. everyone
15. everything

▶ **Make a Switch** Switch the order of the small words to form a compound word. Then write the Spelling Word.

1. case   book   ____bookcase____

2. way   door   ____doorway____

3. out   time   ____timeout____

4. up   pick   ____pickup____

▶ **Word Math** Do word math. Write the Spelling Words.

5. sunflower − 🌼 + set = ____sunset____

6. ☀ + shiny − y + e = ____sunshine____

7. opposite of *down* + **STOP** − op + airs = ____upstairs____

8. 👣 + base − se + ll = ____football____

9. out + 🚪 + s = ____outdoors____

10. ♪♫♩ + look − l + b = ____notebook____

Harcourt

Name _____

VCCV Words

▶ Write Spelling Words to complete the story.

Dad cannot wait **(1)** _____until_____ the cold

(2) _____winter_____ weather goes away. "I will be

happy to **(3)** _____welcome_____ the spring," he **(4)**

_____always_____ says. When spring comes, he plants

a large vegetable **(5)** _____garden_____ . He treats the

young, **(6)** _____tender_____ plants with care.

▶ Write a Spelling Word to match each picture.

7. _____cactus_____

8. _____cowboy_____

9. _____lasso_____

10. _____horses_____

11. _____corral_____

▶ Write the following Spelling Words: *fifteen*, *basket*, *market*, and *Monday*. Use your best handwriting.

12. _____fifteen_____   14. _____market_____

13. _____basket_____   15. _____Monday_____

SPELLING WORDS

1. cowboy
2. horses
3. corral
4. winter
5. always
6. cactus
7. garden
8. tender
9. fifteen
10. basket
11. welcome
12. lasso
13. market
14. until
15. Monday

Handwriting Tip: You will write more clearly if you slant the bottom of the paper toward the elbow of your writing arm and hold the top corner of the paper with your other hand.

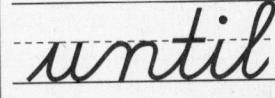

until

Harcourt

SPELLING WORDS

1. cowboy
2. horses
3. corral
4. winter
5. always
6. cactus
7. garden
8. tender
9. fifteen
10. basket
11. welcome
12. lasso
13. market
14. until
15. Monday

SPELLING STRATEGY

Proofread with a Partner

Work with a partner to proofread. Take turns checking for words with the VCCV spelling pattern.

▶ **Work with a partner to circle the six Spelling Words that do not look right. Write the correct spelling for each one.**

1. (wintur)   cactus   _____ winter
2. Monday   (untill)   _____ until
3. (lassoo)   basket   _____ lasso
4. (allways)   cowboy   _____ always
5. corral   (welcom)   _____ welcome
6. fifteen   (tendre)   _____ tender

▶ **Read the schedule. Circle the six misspelled words. Then write the correct spellings on the lines below.**

My Schedule	
Sunday	(Munday)
Buy a (cactis).	Go to the (markit).
Weed the (gardin).	Take a fruit (baskit) to Joe.
Fix the (corall).	

7. _____ cactus   10. _____ Monday

8. _____ garden   11. _____ market

9. _____ corral   12. _____ basket

Harcourt

Name _____

▶ **Edit the Want Ad** Circle the six misspelled words. Write each word correctly below.

Wanted: A (cowboye) needed to train wild (hoarses) in our new (coral). You must be able to use a (lasoe). The pay is (fiftean) dollars a week. Put your name in the (baskit) at our ranch if you want the job.

1. _cowboy_	4. _lasso_
2. _horses_	5. _fifteen_
3. _corral_	6. _basket_

▶ **Silly Sentences** Circle the misspelled word in each sentence. Then write the Spelling Word correctly.

7. July and August are (wintr) months.

winter

8. Don't forget to say "(wellcome)" when you leave! _welcome_

9. Sunday comes after (Munday).

Monday

10. There is a (cactas) on the moon.

cactus

11. I (allways) brush my teeth after I go to bed.

always

12. Robots are growing in our (gardden).

garden

SPELLING WORDS

1. cowboy
2. horses
3. corral
4. winter
5. always
6. cactus
7. garden
8. tender
9. fifteen
10. basket
11. welcome
12. lasso
13. market
14. until
15. Monday

Harcourt

SPELLING WORDS

1. belong
2. hotel
3. focus
4. miner
5. pupil
6. begin
7. music
8. future
9. behind
10. tiger
11. become
12. motel
13. baker
14. cabin
15. ocean

Handwriting Tip: Remember to hold your pencil between your thumb and pointer finger. Let the pencil rest on your middle finger.

_____

ocean

VCV Words

▶ **Write a Spelling Word for each clue.**

1. someone who makes bread ___baker___

2. another word for *sea* ___ocean___

3. a student ___pupil___

4. start ___begin___

5. a large striped cat ___tiger___

6. someone who works underground ___miner___

7. a house in the woods ___cabin___

8. the opposite of past ___future___

▶ **Write a Spelling Word to complete each sentence.**

9. I sat ___behind___ a lady with a tall hat.

10. I could not ___focus___ my tired eyes.

11. We stayed at a ___hotel___ on vacation. Other possible responses: cabin, motel

▶ **Write the following Spelling Words:** *belong, music, become,* and *motel.* **Use your best handwriting.**

12. ___belong___   14. ___become___

13. ___music___   15. ___motel___

Harcourt

Name_____

▶ **Write a Spelling Word in each word shape.
Use the clues to help you.**

1. 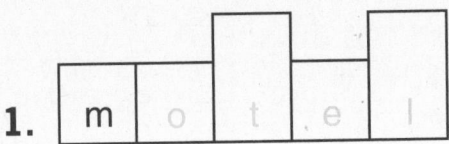 m o t e l

2. 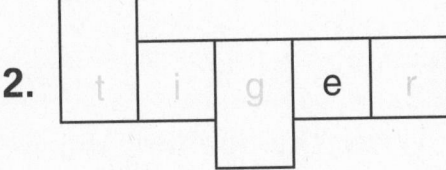 t i g e r

3. 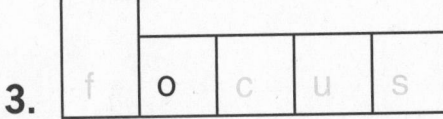 f o c u s

4. 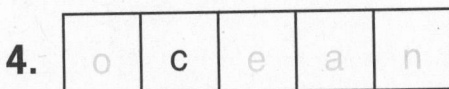 o c e a n

SPELLING WORDS

1. belong
2. hotel
3. focus
4. miner
5. pupil
6. begin
7. music
8. future
9. behind
10. tiger
11. become
12. motel
13. baker
14. cabin
15. ocean

▶ **Read the postcard. Circle the six misspelled
words. Then write the correct spellings on the
lines below.**

What a trip! Our room in the (hotell) is
beautiful. We feel as if we (billong) here.

Tomorrow I will (beginn) my hula lessons. I
just love the (musick) that goes with hula dancing.
Maybe, in the (futcher,) I will (becom) a famous
hula dancer.

5. _____hotel_____   8. _____music_____

6. _____belong_____   9. _____future_____

7. _____begin_____   10. _____become_____

**SPELLING
STRATEGY
Word Shapes**

To remember
the spelling of a
word, draw its
shape.

Harcourt

LESSON 23   **SPELLING PRACTICE BOOK**   **85**

SPELLING WORDS

1. belong
2. hotel
3. focus
4. miner
5. pupil
6. begin
7. music
8. future
9. behind
10. tiger
11. become
12. motel
13. baker
14. cabin
15. ocean

▶ **Opposites** Write the Spelling Words that are the opposite of the underlined words.

1. When will Dad end the story? ___begin___
2. The earth's past is important to everyone.
   ___future___
3. Ron is ahead of Anne in line. ___behind___

▶ **Smaller Words** Write the Spelling Words that have these smaller words in them.

4.–5. us ___music___
      ___focus___

6. hot ___hotel___
7. long ___belong___
8. up ___pupil___
9. an ___ocean___
10. come ___become___
11. cab ___cabin___
12. mine ___miner___
13. bake ___baker___
14. beg ___begin___

Harcourt

Name_____

Words with -ed and -ing

SPELLING WORDS

1. blooming
2. settled
3. stamping
4. leaving
5. liked
6. taking
7. getting
8. filled
9. swimming
10. rolled
11. hoping
12. used
13. hurrying
14. buying
15. worried

▶ **Write Spelling Words to complete the sentences.**

I **(1)** ____liked____ that movie. I kept

(2) ____hoping____ the good guys would win, and they did!

I'm really sad that you're **(3)** ____leaving____.

We were just **(4)** ____getting____ to be friends.

It's too hot outside. How about

(5) ____taking____ a little dip in that

(6) ____swimming____ pool?

▶ **Write a Spelling Word for each clue.**

7. poured to the top ____filled____

8. opening up like a flower ____blooming____

9. going fast ____hurrying____

10. paying for something ____buying____

11. not new ____used____

▶ **Write the following Spelling Words:** *settled, stamping, rolled,* **and** *worried.* **Use your best handwriting.**

12. ____settled____   14. ____rolled____

13. ____stamping____   15. ____worried____

Handwriting Tip: Be sure to leave one pencil space between words and after end punctuation.

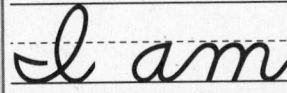

Harcourt

LESSON 24   **SPELLING PRACTICE BOOK**   **87**

SPELLING WORDS

1. blooming
2. settled
3. stamping
4. leaving
5. liked
6. taking
7. getting
8. filled
9. swimming
10. rolled
11. hoping
12. used
13. hurrying
14. buying
15. worried

SPELLING STRATEGY

Word Parts

When you proofread, look for words that end in *-ed* and *-ing*. Think about the base word. Make any necessary spelling changes before you add the endings.

▶ **Add the ending and write the Spelling Word.**

1. worry + ed = _____worried_____
2. settle + ed = _____settled_____
3. get + ing = _____getting_____
4. roll + ed = _____rolled_____
5. use + ed = _____used_____
6. buy + ing = _____buying_____

▶ **Read the letter. Circle the six misspelled words. Then write the correct spellings on the lines below.**

Dear Mom and Dad,

Camp is great. Each day is filld with fun things to do! I likked the hike we took yesterday. I am hopeing we will be takking another one soon. My favorite sport is swiming. I will be sad about leaveing my new friends.

Love,
Becky

7. _____filled_____   10. _____taking_____

8. _____liked_____   11. _____swimming_____

9. _____hoping_____   12. _____leaving_____

Harcourt

Name _____

▶ **Crossword Puzzle** Write Spelling Words to complete this puzzle. Use the clues to help you.

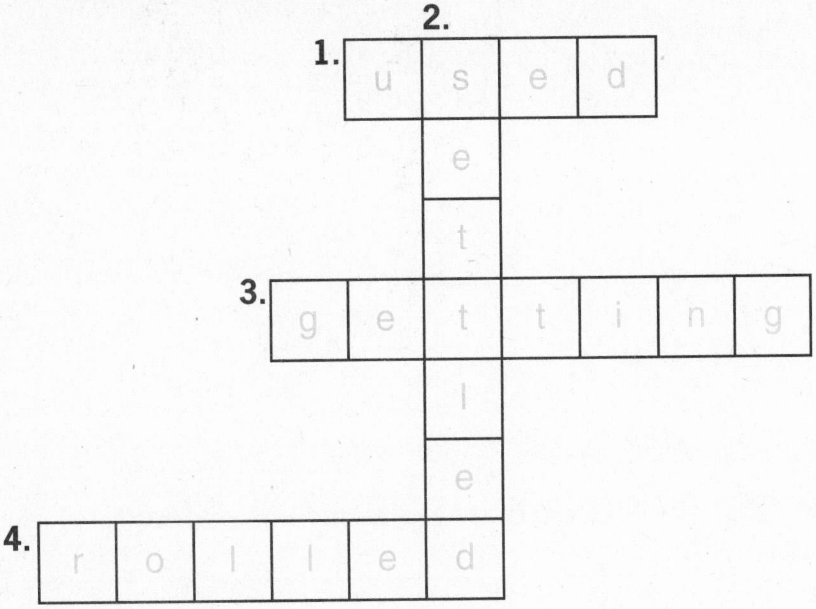

	2.				
1.	u	s	e	d	d

Across down column:
2. s / e / t / t / l / e

3. g e t t i n g

4. r o l l e d

SPELLING WORDS

1. blooming
2. settled
3. stamping
4. leaving
5. liked
6. taking
7. getting
8. filled
9. swimming
10. rolled
11. hoping
12. used
13. hurrying
14. buying
15. worried

1. Mom bought a _____ car.
2. Mr. Santos _____ down for a nap.
3. I am _____ hungry.
4. The puppy _____ around in the leaves.

▶ **Rhyme Time** Complete each sentence with a Spelling Word that rhymes with the underlined word.

5. Birds are <u>zooming</u>, and flowers are

   _____blooming_____.

6. I'll stop <u>worrying</u> if you'll start

   _____hurrying_____.

7. Stop _____stamping_____ your feet right here where we are <u>camping</u>!

8. Who will be <u>flying</u> the plane that she is

   _____buying_____?

Harcourt

SPELLING WORDS

1. combination
2. action
3. vision
4. motion
5. section
6. nation
7. permission
8. confusion
9. question
10. attention
11. vacation
12. production
13. quotation
14. tension
15. sensation

Handwriting Tip: Remember that when an *o* comes before the letter *n*, the *n* begins at the top of both letters, instead of on the bottom line.

-tion

Words with -*tion* and -*sion*

▶ Write a Spelling Word to complete each phrase.

1. a ____permission____ slip

2. a ____section____ of an orange

3. ask a ____question____

4. "Pay ____attention____!"

5. go away on ____vacation____

▶ Put these words in alphabetical order.

production	vision	motion
action	confusion	nation

6. ____action____

7. ____confusion____

8. ____motion____

9. ____nation____

10. ____production____

11. ____vision____

▶ Write the following Spelling Words: *combination*, *quotation*, *tension*, and *sensation*. Use your best handwriting.

12. ____combination____   14. ____tension____

13. ____quotation____   15. ____sensation____

Harcourt

SPELLING PRACTICE BOOK   LESSON 25

Name_____

▶ **Compare the two spellings for each Spelling Word. Circle the word that looks right. Then write the correct spelling for each word.**

1. (quotation)   quotasion   _quotation_

2. visoin   (vision)   _vision_

3. (sensation)   sensasion   _sensation_

4. attension   (attention)   _attention_

5. (nation)   nasion   _nation_

▶ **Circle the seven misspelled words. Then write the correct spellings on the lines below.**

My uncle works at a (mosion) picture studio. He is part of a (producion) crew. During summer (vacasion), we got (permision) to watch him shoot a film. There was so much (confution) and (tention) on the set. Then the director hollered "(Acsion!)" and everyone got to work.

6. _motion_

7. _production_

8. _vacation_

9. _permission_

10. _confusion_

11. _tension_

12. _Action_

SPELLING WORDS

1. combination
2. action
3. vision
4. motion
5. section
6. nation
7. permission
8. confusion
9. question
10. attention
11. vacation
12. production
13. quotation
14. tension
15. sensation

SPELLING STRATEGY

Comparing Spelling

When you proofread, check the spelling of the words that end with *-tion* and *-sion*. If a word does not look right, try writing the word in different ways.

Harcourt

SPELLING WORDS

1. combination
2. action
3. vision
4. motion
5. section
6. nation
7. permission
8. confusion
9. question
10. attention
11. vacation
12. production
13. quotation
14. tension
15. sensation

Name _____

▶ **Putting Words in Their Places** Write the missing Spelling Words to complete each sentence.

(question, attention)

Pay **(1)** ___attention___

when you ask a **(2)** ___question___ .

(vacation, permission)

I had to ask for **(3)** ___permission___

to go on **(4)** ___vacation___ .

(section, vision)

The doctor checked my **(5)** ___vision___ ,

using a **(6)** ___section___ of the chart.

▶ **Putting Things in Order** Put the syllables in order. Then write each Spelling Word correctly.

7. tion na   ___nation___

8. duc pro tion   ___production___

9. fu sion con   ___confusion___

10. tion mo   ___motion___

11. ca tion va   ___vacation___

12. sion vi   ___vision___

13. bin a com tion   ___combination___

14. tion ac   ___action___

Harcourt

Practice Test

▶ **Read each sentence. Fill in the oval next to the correctly spelled word that completes the sentence.**

1. The _____ game will start at 3:00 P.M.

   ⬭ footbal   ⬭ football   ⬭ foot ball

2. Do you laugh _____ for no reason?

   ⬭ sometimes   ⬭ sumtimes   ⬭ some times

3. We invited _____ in the family to the party.

   ⬭ evreone   ⬭ everyone   ⬭ every one

4. They went for a walk on the beach at _____.

   ⬭ sunset   ⬭ sun set   ⬭ sunsett

5. Dan ran _____ to get his coat.

   ⬭ up stairs   ⬭ upstairs   ⬭ upstares

6. Put the boxes in the back of the _____.

   ⬭ pickup   ⬭ pikup   ⬭ pick up

7. What did you do on _____?

   ⬭ Munday   ⬭ Mundy   ⬭ Monday

8. Snow is the best part of _____.

   ⬭ winter   ⬭ wintr   ⬭ wintur

9. A big _____ grows in my yard.

   ⬭ caktus   ⬭ cactis   ⬭ cactus

10. This tomato came from our _____.

   ⬭ guarden   ⬭ garden   ⬭ gardin

▶ **Read each sentence. Find the underlined word that is spelled correctly. Fill in the oval next to the correct spelling.**

1. How does the <u>mussic</u> <u>begin</u>?

   ◯ mussic   ⬭ begin

2. A new <u>pupil</u> sat <u>behinde</u> me today.

   ◯ behinde   ⬭ pupil

3. We stayed in a <u>hotell</u> by the <u>ocean</u>.

   ◯ hotell   ⬭ ocean

4. He <u>liked</u> <u>takeing</u> care of his dog.

   ⬭ liked   ◯ takeing

5. They <u>rolled</u> away the cart <u>filed</u> with pastry.

   ⬭ rolled   ◯ filed

6. We are <u>hopeing</u> he <u>used</u> the right trail.

   ◯ hopeing   ⬭ used

7. We are <u>getting</u> <u>setled</u> in our new home.

   ⬭ getting   ◯ setled

8. He is <u>hurriing</u> to get to the <u>swimming</u> pool.

   ◯ hurriing   ⬭ swimming

9. The man <u>leaveing</u> the room looks <u>worried</u>.

   ◯ leaveing   ⬭ worried

10. You can't sit in <u>section</u> B without <u>permition</u>.

   ⬭ section   ◯ permition

11. The <u>question</u> caused <u>confution</u>.

   ⬭ question   ◯ confution

Harcourt

Name _____

Words with Suffixes

SPELLING WORDS

▶ **Write Spelling Words to complete the story.**

A tractor is a **(1)** ___useful___ machine to a

(2) ___farmer___ . If corn could talk, it would

be very **(3)** ___thankful___ for the rain that falls.

Farming can be a very **(4)** ___lonely___ job. It

is not **(5)** ___suitable___ work for people who

like big cities.

▶ **Write a Spelling Word for each clue.**

6. in a quiet way ___quietly___

7. just right ___exactly___

8. all at once ___suddenly___

9. dangerous ___harmful___

10. an instructor ___teacher___

11. kinder ___nicer___

▶ **Write the following Spelling Words:** *softly,*
readable, safer, **and** *playful.* **Use your best
handwriting.**

12. ___softly___

13. ___readable___

14. ___safer___

15. ___playful___

SPELLING WORDS

1. farmer
2. useful
3. softly
4. suitable
5. lonely
6. quietly
7. teacher
8. thankful
9. exactly
10. readable
11. nicer
12. safer
13. harmful
14. playful
15. suddenly

**Handwriting
Tip:** Make sure
that tall letters,
such as *l, f, b,*
and *d,* touch
both the top and
bottom lines.
Handwriting is
easier to read if
the letters are all
even and take
up the same
amount of space.

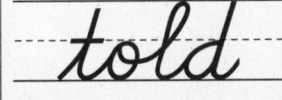
told

SPELLING WORDS

1. farmer
2. useful
3. softly
4. suitable
5. lonely
6. quietly
7. teacher
8. thankful
9. exactly
10. readable
11. nicer
12. safer
13. harmful
14. playful
15. suddenly

SPELLING STRATEGY

Word Parts

When you proofread, look for words with suffixes. Draw a line to separate the base word from the suffix. Check the spelling of the base word, and then add the suffix.

▶ **Add a suffix to write a Spelling Word.**

1. use   _useful_
2. lone   _lonely_
3. suit   _suitable_
4. read   _readable_
5. thank   _thankful_
6. exact   _exactly_
7. soft   _softly_
8. safe   _safer_
9. harm   _harmful_

▶ **Read the journal entry. Circle six misspelled words. Then write the correct spellings on the lines below.**

April 18

Today was a (nisser) day than yesterday. Our (teetcher) was in a (plaful) mood. She let us play (queitly) after lunch. Then she read us a story about a (fahmer) and his magic pitchfork. Then (suddinly) the bell rang. It was time to go home.

10. _nicer_   13. _quietly_
11. _teacher_   14. _farmer_
12. _playful_   15. _suddenly_

Harcourt

Name _____

▶ **Decode the Messages** Unscramble the Spelling Words in each sentence. Then write them correctly.

SPELLING WORDS
1. farmer
2. useful
3. softly
4. suitable
5. lonely
6. quietly
7. teacher
8. thankful
9. exactly
10. readable
11. nicer
12. safer
13. harmful
14. playful
15. suddenly

> The **lolney** rancher was **aukhnflt** to see the letter carrier.

1. _____lonely_____ 2. _____thankful_____

> I don't **clyexta** think those clothes are **iutlabse** for the beach.

3. _____exactly_____ 4. _____suitable_____

> My grandfather is a **rearfm**, and my grandmother is a **caehetr**.

5. _____farmer_____ 6. _____teacher_____

▶ **Try It Out** Add letters to complete the Spelling Words. Then write the words.

7. r e a dab l e _____readable_____

8. q u i et l y _____quietly_____

9. s o f t l y _____softly_____

10. u se f u l _____useful_____

11. s a f e r _____safer_____

12. h a rm f u l _____harmful_____

Harcourt

SPELLING WORDS

1. pennies
2. buried
3. replied
4. candies
5. emptied
6. stories
7. married
8. copies
9. parties
10. studied
11. mysteries
12. discoveries
13. worries
14. families
15. ponies

Handwriting Tip: Keep your letter strokes smooth and steady so your writing will be neat and easy to read. The letters should not be too light or too dark.

copies

Changing *y* to *i*

▶ **Write Spelling Words to complete the story.**

I found a box **(1)** ___buried___ in the garden. It was full of old nickels and **(2)** ___pennies___ . I **(3)** ___emptied___ the coins out on the table. I **(4)** ___studied___ the dates on them. I told my dad about it. He **(5)** ___replied___ , "I guess your great-grandpa put them there. That was about the time he and your great-grandma got **(6)** ___married___ ."

▶ **Write a Spelling Word for each clue.**

7. sweet treats ___candies___

8. things one finds ___discoveries___

9. celebrations ___parties___

10. puzzling tales ___mysteries___

11. small horses ___ponies___

▶ **Write the following Spelling Words:** *copies, stories, worries,* **and** *families.* **Use your best handwriting.**

12. ___copies___   14. ___worries___

13. ___stories___   15. ___families___

Harcourt

Name _____

▶ **Add the ending to write a Spelling Word.**

1. reply + ed   _replied_

2. candy + es   _candies_

3. pony + es   _ponies_

4. marry + ed   _married_

5. worry + es   _worries_

6. party + es   _parties_

▶ **Read the newspaper article. Circle the six misspelled words. Then write the correct spellings on the lines below.**

New Discoverys May Have Solved Old Mystereys

For many years, people have told storys of burried treasure on Alipo Island. Now two familys have found old maps. Some people from the museum studdied the maps. They said the maps are real.

7. _Discoveries_

8. _Mysteries_

9. _stories_

10. _buried_

11. _families_

12. _studied_

SPELLING WORDS

1. pennies
2. buried
3. replied
4. candies
5. emptied
6. stories
7. married
8. copies
9. parties
10. studied
11. mysteries
12. discoveries
13. worries
14. families
15. ponies

SPELLING STRATEGY
Spelling Rules

When you proofread, look for words that have the endings *-ies* and *-ied*. Remember that if a word ends with a consonant and *y*, you change *y* to *i* before adding *-es* or *-ed*.

Harcourt

SPELLING WORDS

1. pennies
2. buried
3. replied
4. candies
5. emptied
6. stories
7. married
8. copies
9. parties
10. studied
11. mysteries
12. discoveries
13. worries
14. families
15. ponies

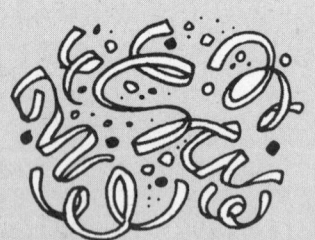

▶ **Picture Sentences** Write a Spelling Word to complete each sentence.

1. Our _____buried_____ his .

2. Three ___pennies___ were left in the .

3. Fran ___emptied___ the .

4. Megan ___studied___ the lesson in her history .

5. Mrs. DeLong made ___copies___ of the map of 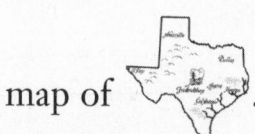 .

▶ **Smaller Words** Write the Spelling Words that have these smaller words in them.

6. and ___candies___
7. my ___mysteries___
8. am ___families___
9. cover ___discoveries___
10. on ___ponies___
11. art ___parties___
12. lied ___replied___

Harcourt

Name _____

Contractions

► **Write a Spelling Word to replace the given words.**

1. Rob would _____ he'd

2. Sue and Kenisha would _____ they'd

3. Rosie is _____ she's

4. You and I have _____ we've

5. You and I would _____ we'd

6. The chair is _____ it's

7. Pedro is _____ he's

► **Write a Spelling Word that is the opposite of the underlined word.**

8. I <u>did</u> finish my homework. _____ didn't

9. It <u>is</u> a warm day today. _____ isn't

10. We <u>will</u> get up early tomorrow. _____ won't

11. I <u>do</u> believe your story. _____ don't

► **Write the following Spelling Words: _you've_, _haven't_, _there's_, and _we'll_. Use your best handwriting.**

12. _____ you've   14. _____ there's

13. _____ haven't   15. _____ we'll

SPELLING WORDS

1. it's
2. isn't
3. you've
4. we'd
5. didn't
6. she's
7. we've
8. haven't
9. he'd
10. they'd
11. there's
12. don't
13. we'll
14. won't
15. he's

Handwriting Tip: When you write contractions, be careful not to join the letter before the apostrophe to the letter after it. Be sure to write the apostrophe at the top of the line.

_he's_

Harcourt

SPELLING WORDS

1. it's
2. isn't
3. you've
4. we'd
5. didn't
6. she's
7. we've
8. haven't
9. he'd
10. they'd
11. there's
12. don't
13. we'll
14. won't
15. he's

SPELLING STRATEGY

Contractions

Check the spelling of contractions. Make sure an apostrophe replaces the letter or letters that you leave out.

▶ **Write each Spelling Word correctly by adding the apostrophe.**

1. theyd   they'd
2. havent   haven't
3. weve   we've
4. its   it's
5. wont   won't
6. didnt   didn't

▶ **Read the note. Circle the six misspelled words. Then write the correct spellings on the lines below.**

Isnt it great that youve gotten a letter from Tim that says hed like to visit? Wed like to see him, too. I read that theres a new pizza place in town. Well have to go there together when Tim comes.

7. _____ Isn't
8. _____ you've
9. _____ he'd
10. _____ We'd
11. _____ there's
12. _____ We'll

Harcourt

Name _____

▶ **Unscramble the Words** Rearrange each group of letters to write a Spelling Word. Remember to add an apostrophe to each word.

<table>
<tr><td></td><td></td></tr>
</table>

1. sehs _____she's_____

2. nodt _____don't_____

3. sti _____it's_____

4. nhvtea _____haven't_____

5. ewd _____we'd_____

6. vwee _____we've_____

7. seh _____he's_____

8. nsit _____isn't_____

▶ **Word Shapes** Write a Spelling Word in each word shape. Use the clues to help you.

9. h e ' d

10. y o u ' v e

11. t h e y ' d

12. d i d n ' t

13. w e ' l l

SPELLING WORDS

1. it's
2. isn't
3. you've
4. we'd
5. didn't
6. she's
7. we've
8. haven't
9. he'd
10. they'd
11. there's
12. don't
13. we'll
14. won't
15. he's

Harcourt

SPELLING WORDS

1. water
2. over
3. never
4. under
5. river
6. number
7. wonder
8. tower
9. rather
10. finger
11. center
12. prefer
13. better
14. border
15. fever

Handwriting Tip: Be careful when writing the letter *e*, or it could look like an *i* and make a correctly spelled word look incorrect.

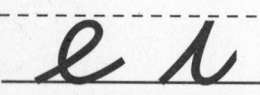

Words That End Like *ever*

▶ **Write Spelling Words to complete the story.**

    The airplane ride was exciting. I could see the

(1) _____river_____ that flows near my house. I

(2) _____never_____ knew it could look so small!

We flew **(3)** _____over_____ mountains and

plains. I could see the trees that run along the

(4) _____border_____ of our land. Then, people in

a control **(5)** _____tower_____ at the airport told

the pilot when to land. I think flying is much

(6) _____better_____ than riding in a car.

▶ **Write a Spelling Word for each clue.**

7. not over   _____under_____

8. to like more   _____prefer_____

9. a high body temperature   _____fever_____

10. the middle   _____center_____

11. a part of a hand   _____finger_____

▶ **Write the following Spelling Words:** *water, number, wonder,* **and** *rather.* **Use your best handwriting.**

12. _____water_____   14. _____wonder_____

13. _____number_____   15. _____rather_____

Harcourt

Name_____

▶ **Write the Spelling Word that best fits with each group of words.**

1. mountain, desert, _____river_____

2. below, beneath, _____under_____

3. no, not, _____never_____

4. wrist, hand, _____finger_____

5. good, _____better_____, best

6. under, beside, _____over_____

▶ **Read the letter. Circle the six misspelled words. Then write the correct spellings on the lines below.**

Dear Grandma and Grandpa,

Did you know that I was sick? Mom said I was feeling undr the weather. I wondre where that saying came from. I did have a high fevre for two days. The doctor told me to drink lots of watter. I drew you a picture of a castle. That's me waving from the towr in the centr of the castle.

Love,

Mike

7. _____under_____   10. _____water_____

8. _____wonder_____   11. _____tower_____

9. _____fever_____   12. _____center_____

SPELLING WORDS
1. water
2. over
3. never
4. under
5. river
6. number
7. wonder
8. tower
9. rather
10. finger
11. center
12. prefer
13. better
14. border
15. fever

SPELLING
STRATEGY
Word Shapes

To remember the spelling of a word, draw its shape.

Harcourt

SPELLING WORDS

1. water
2. over
3. never
4. under
5. river
6. number
7. wonder
8. tower
9. rather
10. finger
11. center
12. prefer
13. better
14. border
15. fever

Name _____

▶ **Change-a-Word** Add and subtract letters from the words below to write Spelling Words.

1. clove – cl + r = _____ over

2. won + d + ear – a = _____ wonder

3. t + show – sh + er = _____ tower

4. r + ate – e + herd – d = _____ rather

5. born – n + deck – ck + r = _____ border

6. anum – a + bed – d + r = _____ number

▶ **Word Shapes** Write a Spelling Word in each word shape.

7.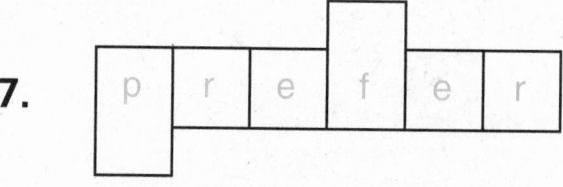
p r e f e r

8.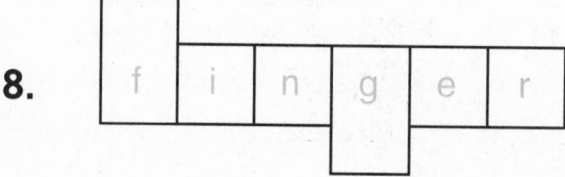
f i n g e r

9.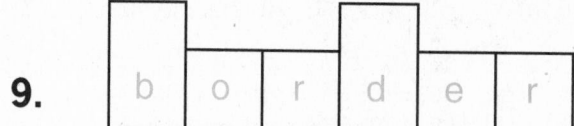
b o r d e r

10.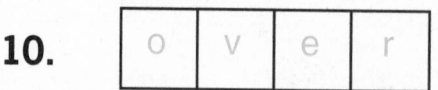
o v e r

11.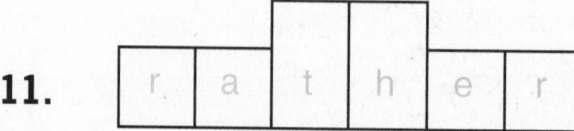
r a t h e r

Harcourt

Words Ending with -le or -al

SPELLING WORDS

1. simple
2. total
3. apple
4. title
5. central
6. purple
7. signal
8. normal
9. middle
10. able
11. terrible
12. people
13. medal
14. handle
15. single

▶ Write a Spelling Word for each clue.

1. center   middle
   _____

2. common   normal
   _____

3. entire   total
   _____

4. easy   simple
   _____

5. noticeable message   signal
   _____

▶ Write a Spelling Word to complete each sentence.

6. What is the ____title____ of the book?

7. The family room is in the ____central____ part of our house.

8. My favorite color is ____purple____.

9. Carry the suitcase by its ____handle____.

10. I was not ____able____ to lift the box.

11. The judge pinned a gold ____medal____ on Leon's shirt.

▶ Write the following Spelling Words: *apple*, *terrible*, *people*, and *single*. Use your best handwriting.

12. ___apple___   14. ___people___

13. ___terrible___   15. ___single___

Handwriting Tip: When you write in small spaces, be sure to keep all tall letters the same height, all short letters the same height, and all letters with tails the same length.

simple

Harcourt

SPELLING WORDS

1. simple
2. total
3. apple
4. title
5. central
6. purple
7. signal
8. normal
9. middle
10. able
11. terrible
12. people
13. medal
14. handle
15. single

SPELLING STRATEGY

Using A Dictionary

Look for words that end in *-le* or *-al* as you proofread. Use a dictionary to check words that do not look right. Dictionary guide words can help you find a word quickly.

▶ **Write the Spelling Words that would appear on the page with the two guide words given.**

nickel	now	1.	normal
meat	mitten	2.	medal
		3.	middle
center	corner	4.	central
paper	purpose	5.	people
		6.	purple

▶ **Read the sign. Circle the six misspelled words. Then write the correct spellings on the lines below.**

Warning: Detour Ahead
Main Street is in terribul shape.
It is not abel to handel traffic today.
Turn right at the next traffic signle onto
Maple Street. Drive in a singal lane.
Take a left at the appel
orchard.

7. terrible   10. signal

8. able   11. single

9. handle   12. apple

Harcourt

Name _____

▶ **Smaller Words** Write the Spelling Words that have these smaller words in them.

1. sign   _____signal_____

2. or   _____normal_____

3. in   _____single_____

4. cent   _____central_____

5. to   _____total_____

6. imp   _____simple_____

▶ **Picture Clues** Write a Spelling Word to match each picture.

7. _____apple_____

10. _____handle_____

8. _____medal_____

11. _____people_____

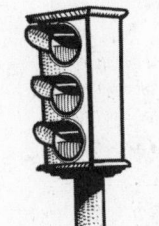

9. _____signal_____

Book of Cats

12. _____title_____

SPELLING WORDS

1. simple
2. total
3. apple
4. title
5. central
6. purple
7. signal
8. normal
9. middle
10. able
11. terrible
12. people
13. medal
14. handle
15. single

Harcourt

Practice Test

▶ Read each sentence. The underlined word is misspelled. Fill in the oval next to the correct spelling.

1. Tell me exactle what you need for your project.

   ⬭ exactly   ⬭ exactlee   ⬭ exectly

2. Our teasher told us a scary story.

   ⬭ teachur   ⬭ teacher   ⬭ teachir

3. Let's find a sootable home for Daisy.

   ⬭ suitabel   ⬭ suitable   ⬭ suitabul

4. How can mice be uzeful?

   ⬭ usefull   ⬭ useful   ⬭ uesful

5. You will be sayfer if you wear a bike helmet.

   ⬭ safer   ⬭ saifer   ⬭ safre

6. The sky sudenly turned dark.

   ⬭ suddnly   ⬭ suddnely   ⬭ suddenly

7. Max beried the turkey bone in the backyard.

   ⬭ buried   ⬭ burried   ⬭ buryed

8. I need two copees of this map.

   ⬭ copeze   ⬭ copies   ⬭ coopies

9. She has lots of pennees in her bank.

   ⬭ penies   ⬭ pennys   ⬭ pennies

10. He empteed his plate twice.

   ⬭ emptied   ⬭ empted   ⬭ emptyed

Harcourt

Name _____

▶ **Read each sentence. Fill in the oval next to the correctly spelled word that completes each sentence.**

1. Do you think _____ got enough time?
   - ⬭ whev'e
   - ⬬ we've
   - ⬭ wea've

2. They said _____ be here by noon.
   - ⬬ they'd
   - ⬭ the'yd
   - ⬭ they'ld

3. She _____ wait for her change.
   - ⬬ didn't
   - ⬭ did'nt
   - ⬭ didnt

4. What is your telephone _____?
   - ⬭ nomber
   - ⬬ number
   - ⬭ numbur

5. This _____ doesn't taste right.
   - ⬬ water
   - ⬭ watur
   - ⬭ watter

6. I _____ who will win first prize.
   - ⬭ wonnder
   - ⬬ wonder
   - ⬭ wunder

7. The _____ was flowing slowly.
   - ⬭ rivar
   - ⬭ rivere
   - ⬬ river

8. The blue skirt is nice, but I _____ the red one.
   - ⬭ preffer
   - ⬭ prafer
   - ⬬ prefer

9. They built a fence along the _____.
   - ⬭ boarder
   - ⬬ border
   - ⬭ boredr

10. I'm looking for a _____ crayon.
    - ⬭ purpal
    - ⬬ purple
    - ⬭ purpel

11. My desk is in the _____ of the room.
    - ⬬ middle
    - ⬭ middal
    - ⬭ midle

Harcourt

Spelling Table

THE SPELLING TABLE below lists all the sounds that we use to speak the words of English. Each first column of the table gives the pronunciation symbol for a sound, such as ō. Each second column of the table gives an example of a common word in which this sound appears, such as *open* for the /ō/ sound. Each third column of the table provides examples of the ways that a sound can be spelled, such as *oh, o, oa, ow, ough, oe,* and *o–e* for the /ō/ sound.

The Sound	As In	Is Spelled As
a	add	cat
ā	age	game, rain, day, paper
ä	palm	ah, father, dark, heart
â(r)	care	dare, fair, where, bear, their
b	bat	big, cabin, rabbit
ch	check	chop, march, catch
d	dog	dig, bad, ladder, called
e	egg	end, met, ready, any, said, says, friend
ē	eat	she, eat, see, people, key, field, city
f	fit	five, offer, cough, photo
g	go	gate, bigger
h	hot	hope, who
i	it	inch, hit, pretty, been, busy
ī	ice	item, fine, pie, buy, high, try, dye, eye
j	joy	jump, gem, magic, cage, edge
k	keep	king, cat, lock
l	look	let, ball

Harcourt

The Sound	As In	Is Spelled As
m	move	**m**ake, ham**m**er
n	**n**ice	**n**ew, ca**n**, fun**n**y, **kn**ow
ng	ri**ng**	thi**ng**, to**ngue**
o	**o**dd	p**o**t, h**o**nor
ō	**o**pen	**oh**, **o**ver, g**o**, **oa**k, gr**ow**, th**ough**, t**oe**, b**o**ne
ô	d**o**g	f**or**, m**o**re, r**oar**, b**a**ll, w**a**lk, d**aw**n, f**au**lt, br**oa**d, **ough**t
oi	**oi**l	n**oi**se, t**oy**
o͝o	t**oo**k	f**oo**t, w**ou**ld, w**o**lf, p**u**ll
o͞o	p**oo**l	c**oo**l, l**o**se, s**ou**p, thr**ough**, d**ue**, fr**ui**t, dr**ew**
ou	**ou**t	**ou**nce, n**ow**
p	**p**ut	**p**in, ca**p**, ha**pp**y
r	**r**un	**r**ed, ca**r**, hu**rr**y, **wr**ist
s	**s**ee	**s**it, **sc**ene, lo**ss**, li**s**ten, **c**ity
sh	ru**sh**	**sh**oe, **s**ure, o**c**ean, spe**ci**al
t	**t**op	**t**an, kep**t**, be**tt**er, walk**ed**, caugh**t**
th	**th**in	**th**ink, clo**th**
t̶h̶	**th**is	**th**ese, clo**th**ing
u	**u**p	c**u**t, b**u**tter, s**o**me, fl**oo**d, d**oe**s, y**ou**ng
û(r)	b**ur**n	t**ur**n, b**ir**d, w**or**k, **ear**ly, h**er**d
v	**v**ery	**v**ote, o**v**er, o**f**
w	**w**in	**w**ait, to**w**el
y	**y**et	**y**ear, on**i**on
yo͞o	**u**se	**c**ue, f**ew**
z	**z**oo	**z**ebra, la**z**y, bu**zz**, wa**s**, s**c**i**ss**ors
zh	vi**si**on	gara**ge**, televi**si**on
ə		**a**bout, list**e**n, penc**i**l, mel**o**n, circ**u**s

Harcourt

Spelling Strategies

Let us show you some of our favorite spelling strategies!

Here's a tip that helps me spell a word. I **say** the word. Then I **picture** the way it is spelled. Then I **write** it!

When I'm learning how to spell a word, the **Study Steps to Learn a Word** are a big help. See pages 8 and 9.

I think of ways to spell the vowel sounds in a word. Then I **try different spellings** until the word looks right.

When I don't know how to spell a word, I sometimes just take my best **guess!** Then I **check** it in a **dictionary**.

Sometimes I **read** the sentences **backward.** I start with the last word and end with the first word. It really helps me notice words I've misspelled! Then I proofread for meaning.

Harcourt

I **proofread** my work **twice.** First, I circle words I know are misspelled. Then, I look for words I'm not sure of.

I look for **homophones** and make sure each word I've written makes sense.

When I'm writing a **compound word,** I think about how the **two smaller words** are spelled.

Sometimes thinking of a **rhyming word** helps me figure out how to spell a word.

I think about **spelling rules,** such as how to change the spelling before adding -ed or -ing.

Drawing the **shape** of a word helps me remember its spelling. This is the shape of the word yellow.

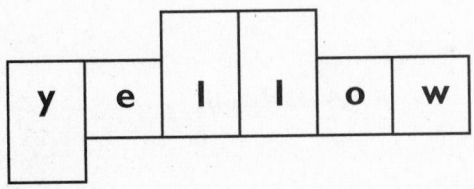

When I **proofread,** I like to **work with a partner.** First, I read the words aloud as my partner looks at the spelling. Then we switch jobs.

My Spelling Log

WHAT'S A SPELLING LOG? It's a special place where you can keep track of words that are important to you. Look at what you'll find in your Spelling Log!

Spelling Words to Study

This is a great place for you to list the words you need to study. There is a column for each unit of your spelling book.

My Own Word Collection

Be a word collector, and keep your collection here! Sort words you want to remember into fun categories you make up yourself!

Sound Words

Cheerful Words

Social Studies Words

Vacation Words

Music Words

Funny Words

Animal Words

Math Words

Harcourt

Spelling Words to Study

List the words from each lesson that need your special attention. Be sure to list the words that you misspelled on the Pretest.

Theme 1	Theme 2
Words with Short *a* and Short *e*	Words with *kn, wr, gh,* and *ph*
Words with Short *i, o,* and *u*	Words with *sh, ch,* and *tch*
Words with Long *a* and *e*	Words with /s/ and /j/
Words with Long *i* and *o*	Words with /oi/
Words with *str* and *st*	Words with /ou/

Harcourt

Spelling Words to Study

Theme 3	Theme 4
Possessives and Plurals	Words with /ôr/
Words with /ô/	Homophones
Words with /o͞o/ and /o͝o/	Words with /ûr/
Words with /är/	Words with Double Consonants
Words with /âr/	Words with -er and -est

Harcourt

Spelling Words to Study

Theme 5	Theme 6
Compound Words	Words with Suffixes
VCCV Words	Changing *y* to *i*
VCV Words	Contractions
Words with *-ed* and *-ing*	Words That End Like *ever*
Words with *-tion* and *-sion*	Words Ending with *-le* or *-al*

Harcourt

My Own Word Collection

When you read and listen, be on the lookout for words you want to remember. Group them into categories any way you like, and write them on these pages. Pretty soon you'll have a word collection of your very own!

Harcourt

My Own Word Collection

Save words you really like in your collection. Include words you have trouble pronouncing or spelling.

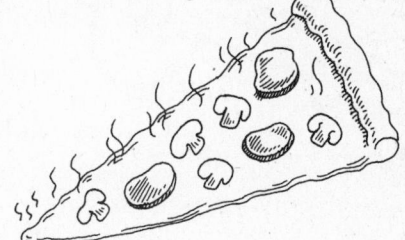

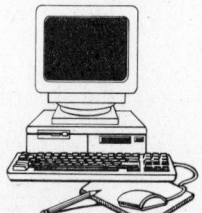

Harcourt

My Own Word Collection

Add a clue beside a word to help you remember it. The clue might be a picture, a sentence, a definition, or just a note.

Harcourt

Handwriting
Manuscript Alphabet

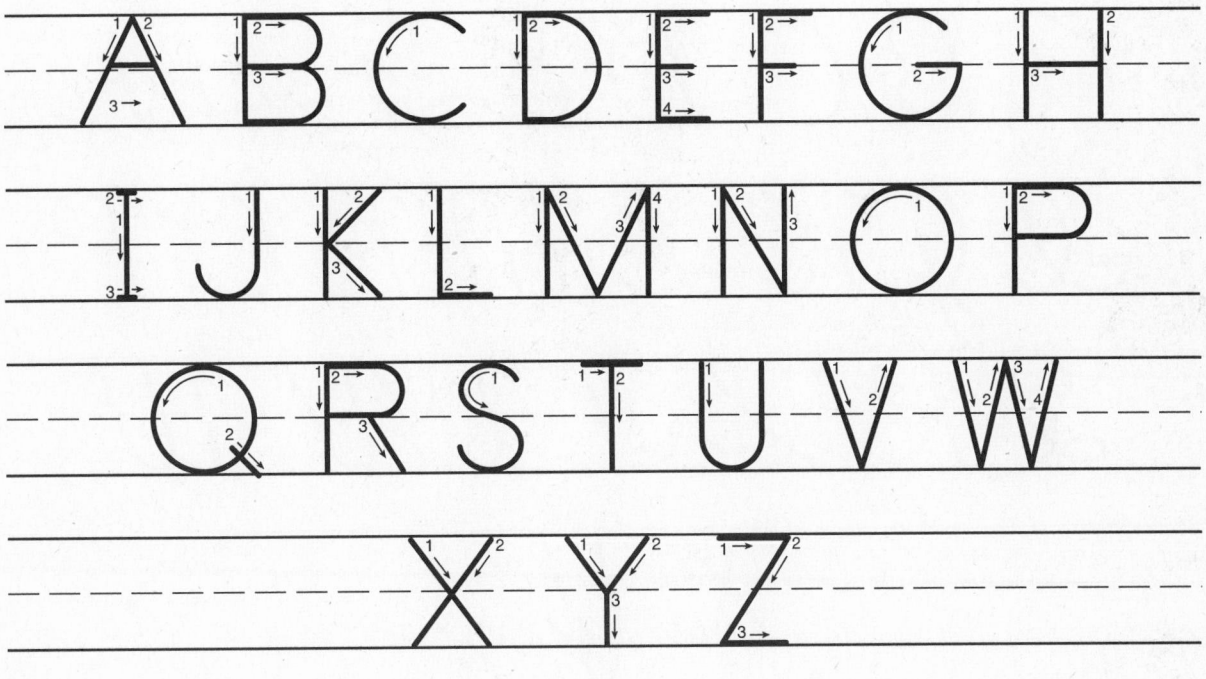

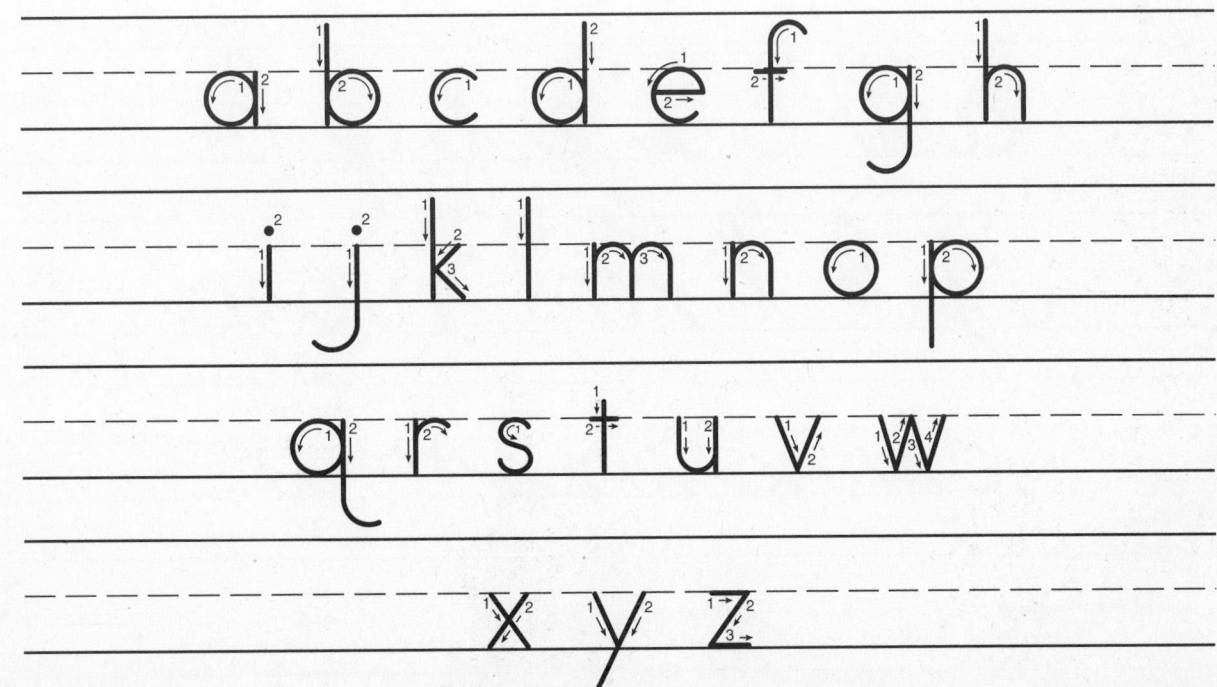

Harcourt

Handwriting
Cursive Alphabet

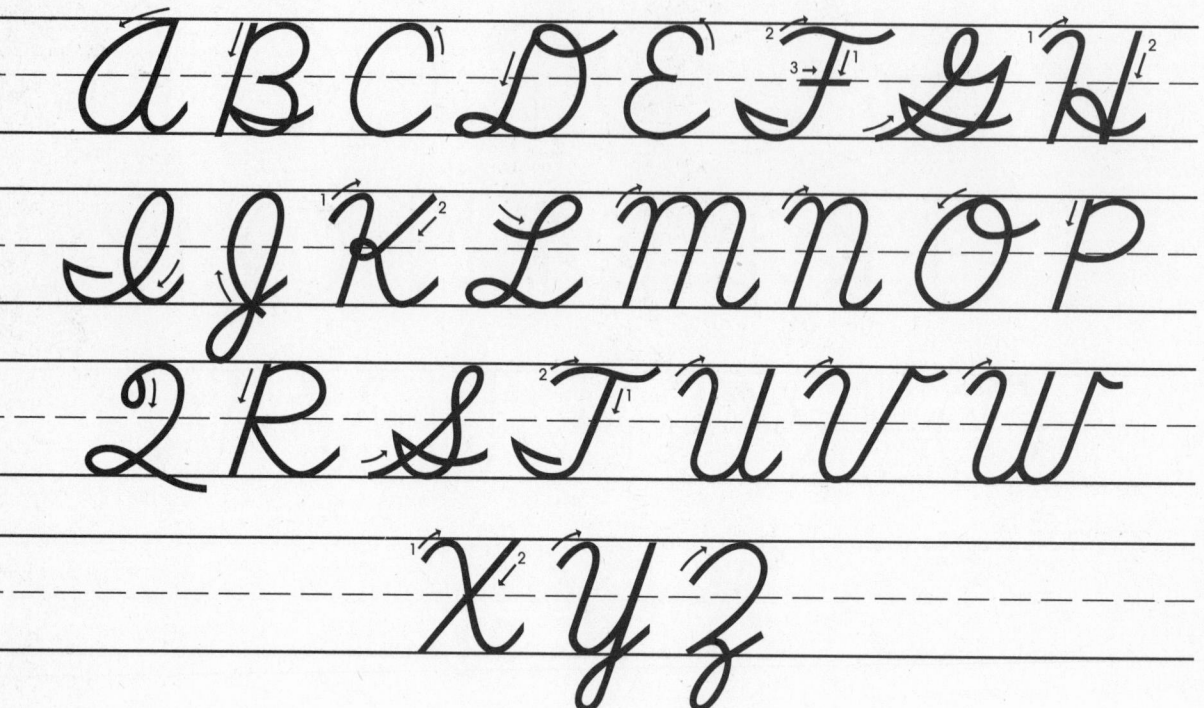

HANDWRITING MODELS

Harcourt

Handwriting
D'Nealian Manuscript Alphabet

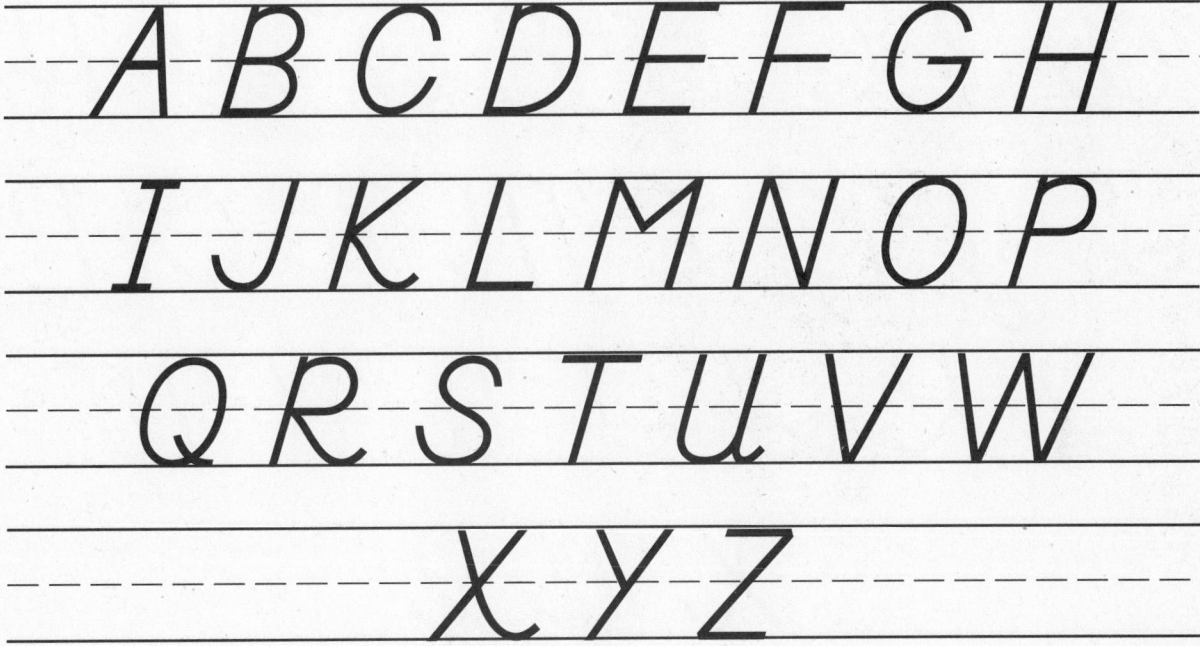

Harcourt

Handwriting
D'Nealian Cursive Alphabet

A B C D E F G H

I J K L M N O P

Q R S T U V W

X Y Z

a b c d e f g h

i j k l m n o p

q r s t u v w

x y z

Harcourt